As someone who knows the joy and value of having been read aloud to as a young person, I have nothing but praise for Sarah Mackenzie and the *Read-Aloud Revival*. Starting with Jim Trelease and *The Read-Aloud Handbook*, Sarah further demystifies—and brings up to speed—the deceptively simple act of reading aloud to young people. It is obvious that Sarah has done the homework. Her insights, suggestions, and enthusiasm are contagious—and they work! Brava, Sarah!

Tomie dePaola, children's book author and artist

The Read-Aloud Family is overflowing with bookish enthusiasm. This book will make you want to sit down and READ—for your own sake, for your kids' sake, for the sake of all the world.

Anne Bogel, creator of ModernMrsDarcy.com and the *What Should I Read Next* podcast, and author of *Reading People: How Seeing the World Through the Lens of Personality Changes Everything.*

In *The Read-Aloud Family*, Sarah Mackenzie has written a true gem. The vetted lists of good books for each age group is priceless in itself. Equally so, Sarah has provided accessible and powerfully written research on why reading aloud is so important to children and families. Sarah is also a natural storyteller. Humanity and family joy rise up off these pages. I highly recommend this book.

Michael Gurian, bestselling author of *Saving Our Sons* and *The Minds of Girls*

Sarah Mackenzie has crafted a treasure of a book that is an answer to every parent's prayer. Delivered with Sarah's signature warmth and relatability, *The Read-Aloud Family* is an accessible guide to the importance of sharing books with those we love. Looking for the true meaning of quality time? Here it is! This practical resource is for anyone who cares deeply about literacy and raising children to become lifelong readers.

Andrea Davis Pinkney, *New York Times* bestselling and Coretta Scott King Award-winning au
Story of Ezra Jack Keats and th

With this marvelous book, Sarah Mackenzie could change your life. We all want our children to be great readers—it will certainly make all the difference in their lives—and Sarah provides an inspiring blueprint for success. She has done us all a great service with this wonderful book.

Ken Ludwig, playwright and author of *How to Teach Your Children Shakespeare*

When I need a boost of inspiration on the whys, hows, and whats on reading books with my kids, I turn to Sarah. She's a trustworthy voice, and with this book, she brings it home to my bookshelf—I'm so glad I now have a way to gather her wisdom whenever I need it. She's my generation of parents' go-to reading resource.

Tsh Oxenreider, founder of TheArtofSimple.net and author of *At Home in the World: Reflections on Belonging While Wandering the Globe*

The Read-Aloud Family is both empowering and freeing. Sarah Mackenzie inspires any mother to invest and influence from right where she is with the simple and transforming joy of reading aloud with her children. I can't wait to see the impact this book has on generations to come.

Ruth Chou Simons, mother of six boys, artist, founder of GraceLaced.com, and bestselling author of *GraceLaced: Discovering Timeless Truths Through Seasons of the Heart*

As a kid, reading aloud with my family changed my life. I can't imagine who I would be without it. In this digital age, I'm so grateful to Sarah Mackenzie and her *Read-Aloud Revival* podcast for motivating thousands of parents to read aloud with their children. Now, in this immensely practical book, she winsomely presents the goals, methods, and principles for reading aloud, while gently waving away common excuses. Her pages also positively overflow with thoughtful recommendations. I expect that my wife and I will be revisiting this book for years to come.

N.D. Wilson, bestselling author of books for kids and adults

What a treasure this book is! *The Read-Aloud Family* is a practical and powerful guide to shaping your family's heartbeat through the gift of reading aloud. Sarah's priceless wisdom will equip and excite you as you deepen your connection with your children page by page. *The Read-Aloud Family* is a must-read!

Lara Casey, author of *Make It Happen* and *Cultivate*

Completely practical and totally inspirational, *The Read-Aloud Family* will move even the most hesitant to give read-alouds a chance. It will surely serve as a reference when I have my own family!

Jonathan Bean, award-winning author and illustrator

This wonderful book delights, inspires, and clearly articulates such an important philosophy: that every child should grow up swimming in imagination of great tales and stories remembered! Highly recommended for all parents!

Sally Clarkson, blogger, podcaster and author of many bestselling books, including *The Lifegiving Home*, *Different*, *Educating the WholeHearted Child*, and *Own Your Life*

Three cheers for Sarah Mackenzie! Some of my best memories as a father involve a fireplace, a cozy blanket, and my family hushed by the power of a good story being read aloud. It may sound like a stretch, but I actually believe the world would be a better place if we took the words of Sarah's book to heart.

Andrew Peterson, singer, songwriter, and author of The Wingfeather Saga

I've devoured books since I was a child, but passing that hunger to learn along to my children is less natural than I expected. Then I found Sarah Mackenzie. She equips book lovers to raise our children to be voracious readers and voracious learners—and walks us through how to start, even from as early as when they can fold themselves into our laps. As an avid reader and an author and a mom who has filled the rooms of our house with books: what you have found here is GOLD.

Sara Hagerty, author of Every *Bitter Thing Is Sweet* and *Unseen: The Gift of Being Hidden in a World that Loves to be Noticed*

Sarah's friendly voice extends an invitation to all parents to enjoy sharing stories with our children. No guilt, just inspiration and encouragement. Amid the feast of enthusiasm and abundant resources, Sarah deftly weaves in practical wisdom on how to talk to our kids, not just about books, but about life. I eagerly recommend this book!

S. D. Smith, author of The Green Ember series

The Read-Aloud Family is an absolute gold mine for book lovers, with treasures on each page that will enrich your family for years to come. I've already used so many of Sarah's fresh inspirational tips, and I know I'll return to this title again and again over the years. It's my new favorite baby shower gift!

Jamie C. Martin, co-founder of SimpleHomeschool.net and author of *Give Your Child the World: Raising Globally Minded Kids One Book at a Time*

Jam-packed with lists, tools, strategies and lessons, *The Read-Aloud Family* is a treasured volume worth dogearing for years to come. Whether your kids are two or twenty-two, let Sarah Mackenzie guide you through the power of the family story—both in the books you read and in the life you lead. A true handbook for togetherness.

Erin Loechner, author of *Chasing Slow* and blogger at DesignforMankind.com

The Read-Aloud Family

ALSO BY SARAH MACKENZIE

Teaching from Rest: A Homeschooler's
Guide to Unshakable Peace

The Read-Aloud *Family*

MAKING MEANINGFUL AND LASTING CONNECTIONS WITH YOUR KIDS

SARAH MACKENZIE,
Founder of READ-ALOUD REVIVAL

ZONDERVAN

The Read-Aloud Family
Copyright © 2018 by Sarah Mackenzie

Requests for information should be addressed to:
Zondervan, *3900 Sparks Dr. SE, Grand Rapids, Michigan 49546*

ISBN 978-0-310-35137-5 (ebook)

Library of Congress Cataloging-in-Publication Data

Names: Mackenzie, Sarah, 1981- author.
Title: The read-aloud family : making meaningful and lasting connections with
    your kids / Sarah Mackenzie.
Description: Grand Rapids, MI : Zondervan, [2018] | Includes bibliographical
    references and index.
Identifiers: LCCN 2017056935 | ISBN 9780310350323 (softcover)
Subjects: LCSH: Oral reading. | Reading--Parent participation. | Education--
    Parent participation.
Classification: LCC LB1573.5 .M28 2018 | DDC 372.45/2--dc23 LC record
    available at https://lccn.loc.gov/2017056935

Published in association with William K. Jensen Literary Agency, 119 Bampton
Court, Eugene, Oregon 97404.

Cover design: Curt Diepenhorst
Cover illustration: Daria Kirpach
Interior design: Kait Lamphere

First printing January 2018 / Printed in the United States of America

23 24 25 26 27 LBC 22 21 20 19 18

For my children, who taught me to love reading aloud: Audrey, Allison, Drew, Clara Jane, Emerson, and Becket. May stories always bind us in love.

And for my brother, who passed on to life eternal while I wrote this book. You are forever missed and loved, Nate. *Eternal rest grant unto him O Lord, and let the perpetual light shine upon him.*

• • • •

But the world is a bit short on good fairies these days. So who is to take their place? Who is to make sure that our children's sense of wonder grows indestructible with the years? We are. You and I.

Katherine Paterson, *A Sense of Wonder*

CONTENTS

PART 3: Meeting Them Where They Are

PART 1

The Time Is Now

Chapter 1

HOW READING ALOUD CAN CHANGE THE WORLD

(Or, at least, how it's changing mine)

• • • •

> No one will ever say, no matter how good a parent he or she was, "I think I spent too much time with my children when they were young."
>
> Alice Ozma, *The Reading Promise*

It was just an ordinary Tuesday, really, but it turned out to be so much more than that.

I was twenty years old; it had been a long, rainy spring; and the 450-square-foot apartment my husband and I shared was feeling even more cramped than usual. I packed up our one-year-old daughter, an overstuffed diaper bag, and a cantaloupe in danger of turning too soft, and headed out the door.

When we arrived at my friend's house twenty-five minutes later, Christina opened the front door, threw her arm around my neck, and ushered us into her large, cheery home. I breathed a small sigh of relief and dropped the diaper bag by the stairs—another boring afternoon in our tiny apartment had been successfully averted.

Audrey, my daughter, immediately set off, eager to find the toy box. I trailed her, unzipping her coat as she toddled away. Christina's own toddler, not too keen on me yet, returned my smile with a scowl.

Christina went into the kitchen to dig through the fridge, and I followed her. We had bonded months earlier over birth stories and coffee at a local playgroup, and I was grateful that even though there was at least a decade between my age and Christina's, we could swap fears and feelings as first-time moms.

"Wanna keep an eye on the little ones?" she asked. "I'll just whip up a little something for our lunch."

I wandered to the family room, keeping watch as the toddlers ransacked the toy bins. Just as I was about to drop onto the deep leather sofa, I saw it—a book resting precariously on the edge of the fireplace mantle, Post-its jutting out every which way from the pages. I snatched it up and noted the title: *The Read-Aloud Handbook* by Jim Trelease.

If this had been happening in a movie, I'm certain there would have been music. In fact, it would have been the tension-building part of the soundtrack. The part that helps the movie-watcher realize that something of great importance is happening, that the rest of the story hinges on this seemingly insignificant moment.

At the time, however, all I heard was the babbling of toddlers and the sizzling of the bratwurst Christina was sautéing for lunch. I flipped through the book, noting how many pages were dog-eared, how many were marked up with penciled comments.

"What do you think of this book?" I asked Christina over my shoulder.

She turned from the stove and leaned forward, squinting slightly, to see what I was holding, "Oh, that one? It's great!"

Turning back to her task, she added, "You can borrow it, if you like."

(This is your cue to raise the volume on the soundtrack.)

BEYOND COMPARE

I took Christina's copy of *The Read-Aloud Handbook* home, but I didn't so much read it as inhale it. This alone wasn't terribly unusual—I read voraciously as a new parent. I had big, idealistic dreams for Audrey and for myself—for the kind of mother I wanted to be. I knew just enough to realize I had no clue how to do this well, so I did what I had always done when I was shooting for an A+: I read.

In those early days of parenting, I rarely made decisions without consulting a book. I read books about what to feed my baby, how to encourage her to nap, what to do for her brain development. The stakes were high, and I was determined to rise to meet them.

One dark evening during her first year, Audrey just would *not* fall asleep. It had become a recurring problem and, fearful that *I* was to blame for her poor sleeping habits, I gathered up every parenting book I could find. Spreading them out around me, I sat cross-legged on the apartment floor and searched desperately for a solution to our bedtime struggles. Audrey crawled around me as I sobbed, flipping from one book to the next, wondering why they all gave such conflicting advice and unsure which one to trust. (Fifteen years and five babies later, I wish I could tell my younger self to relax and trust my instincts! Alas, some lessons must be learned through time and experience.)

But even my desire to end the bedtime struggles paled in comparison to the desire I felt to form a meaningful relationship with Audrey. Jim Trelease's idea that reading with my child could be one of the most important building blocks to a lasting and healthy relationship between the two of us intrigued me. Of all things, I wanted to get *this* right.

The Read-Aloud Handbook has sold well over a million copies to date, so I think it's safe to say that I was just one of many whose attention was captured by its message. It presented a new idea for me: the primary goal of reading to children—and of teaching them to read—is not so they can eventually learn to read on their own.

Trelease's book is chock-full of statistics and data that prove reading aloud connects and bonds families and helps kids grow to be successful in just about every area of life, especially in school. In the book, he asserts that read-alouds are the foundation for the close bonds between parents and kids, between teachers and students.

The 1985 Commission on Reading declared, "The single most important activity for building the knowledge required for eventual success in reading is reading aloud to children."[1] Trelease unpacks this, then tells about the astonishing power reading aloud has to build a child's vocabulary, sow the seeds of reading desire, and help kids continue to love books well into their adolescence and beyond.

He proposes read-alouds as the antidote to academic struggle—and not just read-alouds for kids who can't read yet. Read-alouds for babies in the womb, for newborns who don't yet hold up their heads, for toddlers and preschoolers and grade-schoolers and even for teens who are quite capable of reading on their own. Trelease advocates reading aloud to kids *especially* when they can read for themselves. He goes so far as to say that if teachers and parents experience a shortage of time and can't fit in reading aloud, they should "steal [time] from other subjects that are not as essential as reading, which includes pretty much everything else."[2]

The idea that reading aloud should take priority over other things—that even teachers in schools should shuttle other subjects off the schedule to make more room for it—was new to me. As a child, of course, I loved being read to. My favorite part of elementary school was in the first grade, during the fifteen-minute period after lunch recess when the teacher would read to us from Beverly Cleary's *The Mouse and the Motorcycle*. I looked forward to that read-aloud session every single day.

Now, as a brand-new parent, reading board books with Audrey was one of my favorite ways to spend time with her. Of all the tasks and responsibilities associated with parenting, reading was the easiest and most enjoyable. That it could be as profoundly important as Jim Trelease asserted both astonished and delighted me.

That night, I snuggled in next to Audrey and watched her breathe in and out, little puffs of air catching a wisp of her hair as she slept. I turned the pages of *The Read-Aloud Handbook*, and something deep inside me rumbled.

Then, in that moment, I realized my relationship with this child was the most important thing in my life. Nothing else could compare to the bond between this tiny human being and myself. If reading aloud was going to be the best way to nurture that bond, then by golly, I knew what I was going to do.

NO GUARANTEES

I had high hopes for Audrey right out of the gate. I knew that I wanted her to grow up to love God with all of her heart, mind, and soul. I wanted her to do well in school. I wanted a warm relationship with her, always. I wanted her to be kind and compassionate, to do what was right even when no one was looking.

I also knew that with parenting, there are no guarantees. Kids are not recipes, and just because we prepare them or raise them in a particular way doesn't mean they'll turn out how we hope they will. I've known plenty of loving, all-in parents whose grown children always seem to be running a gamut of mistakes and missteps. Kids are human, and humanity is messy. I knew right there at the beginning that my own mothering prowess wouldn't ensure my children would embrace my Christian beliefs, get into good colleges, or make life choices I would be proud of.

• • • • • •

Kids are not recipes, and just because we prepare them or raise them in a particular way doesn't mean they'll turn out how we hope they will.

In parenting, we aren't guaranteed any of that, but I still felt keenly the desire and drive to give Audrey my very best. To stack the odds in favor of her becoming the kind, capable, and loving person I hoped she would be.

All the time and effort it would take to raise her would be worth it—not because it guaranteed good results, but because loving and connecting with her would *always* be worth my time and effort. Because she was mine. Because she was made by God. Because this was the great task I'd been called to.

What I didn't know, as I stroked her cheek and considered the trajectory my life had taken at such a young age, was that five siblings would join her in the next dozen years. Loving and connecting with my kids would become both the greatest challenge and the most thrilling privilege of my life. Parenting would be so very much harder than I could have possibly imagined in those first years, and so much more rewarding.

I did know this one thing, even back then: there was a lot I could get wrong. And oh, how I desperately wanted to get it right.

MY GREATEST FEAR

The possibility that one day my children will be grown and gone and I might regret the choices I made while raising them terrifies me. We only have a certain amount of time available to us, after all. How we choose to spend that time has significant consequences in that it affects how our children live out the rest of their lives. That's daunting.

I'm in the thick of things, and if you're reading this book, I bet you are too. As this book goes to press, my six (yep, six) kids span ages from preschool to high school.

Audrey, that toddling girl who accompanied me, a ripe cantaloupe, and a diaper bag on a visit to Christina's house so many years ago, is entering her final years at home. I'm acutely aware of how easy it is to slip into the habit of just surviving the day, focusing on getting through. I want to make a meaningful and lasting bond with each of my kids before it's too late.

As a busy mother, I struggle to truly connect with each of my kids in a way that will stand the test of time. There's a whole household to tend to, dinner to make, a pile of laundry always spilling into the hallway. Life feels constantly hurried and over-full. School, work, church, extracurricular activities, sports, family affairs, housework, errands. So many things to do. Emails, phone calls, text messages. So much noise.

So. much. noise.

It's just too easy to let these precious childhood years scream by. They *are* screaming by, and I can hardly stop them.

N. D. Wilson words it perfectly in his book *Death by Living*: "Watching one's small humans age and grow up packs a serious punch. It's like being stuck in a dream unable to speak, like being a ghost that can see but not touch, like standing on a huge grate while a storm rains oiled diamonds, like collecting feathers in a storm. Parents in love with their children are all amnesiacs, trying to remember, trying to cherish moments, ghosts trying to hold the world."[3]

That's me—trying to hold the world, trying desperately to catch the oiled diamonds as they fall. Beyond wanting to do a good job at this parenting thing, I want to *enjoy* raising my children. I don't want to look back twenty years from now and realize that those active parenting years went by so fast I didn't relish them. I'm terrified I'll wish I had been less distracted and more attentive. I'm afraid I'll come to the realization, when it's too late, that I should have been more present. I'm afraid I'll wish I had enjoyed it more.

The days I have to raise my children while they are still under my roof, and the days you have to raise yours, are finite. When you picked up this book, you may have thought you were getting a manifesto on reading aloud. By the end of it, you might decide that's exactly what it is.

• • • • •

I want to make sure you know what this book is really about: it's about you and me going all-in for our kids.

But right here at the beginning, I want to make sure you know what this book is really about: it's about you and me going all-in for our kids. It's about doing what matters most with our time and energy today. Right now. Right when it matters most—as diamonds rain down and fall through the grate beneath our feet.

THE BIRTH OF A REVIVAL

Some years after that day at Christina's, I stood on a stool in my kitchen wearing yoga pants, earbuds inserted, scrub brush in hand. Determined to clean out all the kitchen cupboards, I shooed the three kids out to the yard to play with friends while I tackled the silverware drawers and pantry shelves.

I was listening to Andrew Pudewa, president of the Institute for Excellence in Writing, give a talk called "Nurturing Competent Communicators." A friend who heard Pudewa speak at a home-schooling conference was inspired, motivated, and filled with fresh enthusiasm and confidence. I had barely begun my own homeschooling journey, but I was already feeling overwhelmed and in over my head. I thought I could certainly use some of that fresh enthusiasm.

I listened and scrubbed as Pudewa told a crowd of home-schooling parents that the best way to help children grow to be good communicators was to read aloud to them as much as possible and to have them memorize poetry. I wiped crumbs into my hand and remembered *The Read-Aloud Handbook,* inhaled all those years ago. Maybe Pudewa was on to something.

I already read aloud bedtime stories and school books to my kids—especially to my youngest two, who couldn't yet read anything by themselves. But something about Pudewa's talk that day sparked an ember that had lain dormant, buried deep within me. I got to the end of the lecture and started it all over again, vacuuming out corners of drawers and scrubbing honey splatters as I listened once more.

This, I thought to myself. *There's something about this.*

Have you ever seen a campfire that has burned down but not

been completely tamped out? It looks like nothing is happening, but all you have to do is add a small bit of the right fuel—a scrap of paper, a dry piece of kindling, a tiny blast of oxygen—and that fire roars right back to life.

That's exactly what happened when I listened to Andrew Pudewa. I began to read aloud to my three children (then ages eight, six, and four) more than ever. So startling were the results—so completely transformative were the changes in our family—that five years and three more babies later, I could barely keep myself from bubbling over with the thrill of it.

I had an active blog and had begun to play with the idea of starting a podcast. I loved listening to podcasts myself and thought it might be fun to launch one. In a moment of pure impulse in March of 2014, I shot an email off to the Institute for Excellence in Writing: *Would Mr. Pudewa like to come talk with me on a podcast about the importance of reading aloud?*

Within hours I had received a response from his marketing director—yes, Mr. Pudewa would be delighted to be featured on my podcast.

Hmm, I thought, eyeing my nine-month-old twins as they scooted themselves across the floor, *I guess I'd better figure out how to start a podcast.*

It turns out that "how to start a podcast" is, in fact, a valid Google search. I ordered a microphone and headset, created a Skype account, and watched an online tutorial about how to edit voice recordings. I marked the day of the scheduled interview with Andrew Pudewa in bright yellow highlighter on my wall calendar, but as the day drew closer, I became more and more uneasy.

On the day of the interview, my stomach churned. I fired a text to my friend, Pam: *What was I thinking when I asked ANDREW PUDEWA to be on my show? I don't even have a show! I'm going to be sick. This is a bad idea. It was ALWAYS a bad idea. Whose idea was this anyway? See, this is where my rash and impulsive enthusiasm gets me. In too deep.*

Pam responded with just three words: *You'll be fine.*

(She's heartless. Or I suppose she's used to receiving such texts from me. I'll let you decide for yourself.)

The interview went better than I could have hoped (so I guess, in the end, Pam was right), and Mr. Pudewa was a delightful and talkative guest. To this day, I doubt he realizes how terrified I was.

A week later, in between diaper changes and never-ending loads of laundry, I released the *Read-Aloud Revival* podcast. I was certain the internet radio show would last for only a few episodes and provide a very small circle of my blog readers with some encouragement to read more with their kids

I could never have imagined in those first days of the podcast that the show would grow to become what it is today—never dreamed it would see millions of downloads in the first few years and be heard by tens of thousands of families all over the world. As the podcast grew and responses from listeners rolled in, I realized something beautiful: I wasn't alone. Other families had taken to heart this idea that reading aloud could transform their homes, and they had amazing stories to tell about it. Finding other families who were prioritizing books and read-aloud sessions in the way my own family was made my heart sing.

Emails began to fill my inbox. Listeners wrote in to tell me that they were reading aloud with their kids, and that it had become everyone's favorite time of day. They would say that ever since they started listening to the podcast, they had begun reading together before bed, or at lunchtime, or by listening to audiobooks in the car. Their families suddenly had their own inside jokes, their own shared experiences. It was knitting them together in new ways. They told of their nonreading kids who were begging for "one more chapter," of an energy and enthusiasm in their homes the likes of which they had never seen before. Something big was happening in homes all over the world. A revival was taking shape.

In all the conversations I've had on the Read-Aloud Revival podcast with experts, authors, moms, dads, and reading enthusiasts, I've come to understand something that both delights and relieves me: reading aloud with our kids is indeed the best use of our time and energy as parents. It's more important than just about anything else we can do.

> Reading aloud with our kids is indeed the best use of our time and energy as parents. It's more important than just about anything else we can do.

Reading aloud may seem too simple to make that big of an impact. But the stories I've heard over the years from families all over the world, the data collected by experts, and the personal experience I've had sharing stories with my own six kids has convinced me beyond a shadow of a doubt.

WHO KNEW? (WELL, BESIDES JIM TRELEASE)

It turns out I was right all those years ago when I lay, curled up with Audrey, wondering about the mystery of parenthood, about the magnitude of the significant work before me: there are no guarantees. But that doesn't matter—not really. We aren't going all-in for our kids because we are promised excellent results. We're doing it because they mean more to us than anything in the world. When it comes right down to it, we want our children to live out the fullness of God's vision for their lives, and we're willing to do just about anything it takes to stack the odds in favor of that happening.

I wish I could go back and whisper a little something into the ear of twenty-year-old Sarah—back to that fateful day when I stumbled across *The Read-Aloud Handbook* in Christina's living room. I would sidle up next to my new-mom self, offering her a latte and a break from the baby for a few hours.

Then I would tell her, with a sparkle in my eye and a fire in my belly, "Pick up a book. Pull her onto your lap. Read aloud. You will never, ever regret the time you spend reading with your daughter."

• • • • • •

We aren't going all-in for our kids because we are promised excellent results. We're doing it because they mean more to us than anything in the world.

I finished that first reading of *The Read-Aloud Handbook* late at night—long past when I should have been asleep. I turned the last page, put the book down next to me on the bed, and pulled the covers up a little tighter around my chin. Gazing at the ceiling of our postage-stamp apartment, I wondered if he was right, this Jim Trelease.

Could reading aloud change Audrey's life? Could it truly make such an enormous difference in her future? Was it possible that reading books together could bond us with a shared experience to last a lifetime?

My twenty-year-old self didn't know the answer yet. I envisioned myself reading to Audrey at two years old, at eight, at twelve. I pictured myself reading to her at sixteen. And you know what? I liked what I saw. Two people embarking on a journey, hand in hand—seeking adventure, going new places, setting out for the unknown—doing it all together, and all through the pages of a book. Mother and child cuddled up on a sofa or sprawled out on the floor, setting out to see what they could experience by reading stories together. I thought about how having such encounters alongside my child could impact both of us forever. I wanted that for Audrey. I wanted that for me. I wanted that for *us*.

As I lay huddled under the covers that night, it seemed to me that Jim Trelease was saying that reading aloud had the power to change the world. What I never could have predicted was how it was about to transform mine.

WAITING FOR THE WALRUS

Being Fully Present

• • • •

> So as a mother and as a writer, let me urge you to read to them, read to them, read to them. For if we are careless in the matter of nourishing the imagination, the world will pay for it. The world already has.
>
> Katherine Paterson, *A Sense of Wonder*

It was an overcast day, typical for the Pacific Northwest. Nonetheless, I zipped the three kids into their coats and bundled them off to the local zoo, as was our weekly custom, sun or no sun.

"Which animal would you like to see today?" I asked as we pulled into the nearly empty parking lot. I loved days like this— weekday mornings in early spring, with just enough dampness and drizzle to stave off most visitors. Always eager for a change of scenery myself, I gladly accepted the reprieve from being cooped up at home, even with the chill in the air.

"The walrus?" seven-year-old Audrey suggested from the back seat. "We haven't seen that one yet."

I nodded. A good plan. Gathering up our things, I fished in my wallet for our zoo membership card and led my kids through the entrance.

I had seen the walrus before and was eager to watch my children's reactions to their own first encounter with the creature. No matter how often I had seen photos in magazines or watched coverage in documentaries on TV, I was always a little taken aback by the wide eyes of the tiger, the curved trunk of the elephant, the roundness of a snake's belly. I was sure my kids would feel this same sense of awe and wonder today. After all, the first time *I* had seen the walrus, I was transfixed, wondering how such an enormous beast could move so elegantly through the water.

We made our way slowly to the northwest corner of the park, pausing briefly to watch the playful meerkats and peek in on the napping red wolf. By the time we arrived at the walrus exhibit, five-year-old Allison (always the first of my kids to tire) dropped to the ground and let out a dramatic sigh.

The exhibit looked empty, but I knew this was a creature we'd have to be patient to see. The walrus only came to the main viewing area when it pleased. Much of its time was spent in the private corners of its tank.

Audrey and Drew kicked stones around on the pavement, and I gladly set down the backpack, which was heavy with water bottles, sketchbooks, and colored pencils. A seagull landed nearby, plucking the remnants of a soft pretzel from the ground. Allison shimmied toward the walrus tank and sat up on her knees, nose to the glass.

Then it happened. Rippling water signaled movement within the tank. A smile played at my lips, and I called the other two kids to where Allison and I waited.

"It's coming!" I told them. "See the water rippling?"

We peered through the glass eagerly. Just as the magnificent beast burst into view, Allison cried out gleefully, "Oh Mommy, look!"

I turned to her in expectation, eager to watch her first impression of the walrus's size and grace, but instead saw that she wasn't looking through the glass at all. She was on her hands and knees, nose inches from the sidewalk and eyes open wide in amazement, watching an ant skitter across the ground as it carried a piece of food bigger than itself.

In my eagerness to see the walrus, I'd just about let the miracle of a small, ordinary ant carrying a parcel of food larger than itself pass unnoticed. I am 100 percent sure I would have missed it, had Allison not called the miracle of the ant to my attention.

Allison has always been my observer. Quieter than the rest of us, she catches details everyone else seems to steamroll past. She once said, as I was rushing her out the door on a quick trip to the grocery store, "Mommy, slow down—you're moving too fast for my insides!"

That chilly spring day at the zoo nearly a decade ago, I saw my slack-jawed daughter watch an ant cross the sidewalk with rapt attention. She heard nothing, saw nothing, noticed nothing—nothing except for the tiny miracle before her.

Oh, how my heart longs to do the same.

WHAT MATTERS MOST

These days of parenting my kids—days filled with laundry, math homework, Crock-Pot dinners, sand on the entryway rug, piano lessons, soccer practice, orthodontist appointments, grocery runs, sleepovers, and toddlers with the stomach flu—these are days filled with ant moments.

We aren't making weekly treks to the zoo anymore, but I still find myself waiting for those big, splashy, take-my-breath-away moments. I'm waiting for the walrus. And as I do, I'm missing every other miracle.

If you are reading this book, I bet that you, like me, desire to form meaningful and lasting relationships with your kids. I bet that you, like me, hope that when your kids are all grown up, they'll still want to come home for Christmas.

I have twice as many kids today as I did on that overcast day at the zoo, but in some ways, not much has changed. I still find myself waiting for the walrus. I still gloss over the ordinary by default. I'm still plagued by the fear I struggled with so often back then—the fear that I don't have enough time to give my children all that they need, that I'm missing my chance to do what matters most. I feel endlessly distracted by all the other parts of raising kids, and I wonder if, twenty years from now, I'll look back and want to shake myself awake to say, "Pay attention! You're missing this and it's right in front of you!"

This parenting gig is exceedingly important—you and I both know that. If making meaningful and lasting connections with our kids requires that we be fully present and that we focus on what matters most, then there's one question we need to answer for ourselves: *What matters most?* Those myriad distractions aren't going anywhere, so we have to get crystal-clear on where our time and energy are best spent.

In other words, we have to figure out how to notice those ants on the sidewalk—the tiny, miraculous moments we tend to step right over in search of the walrus. If we can do that, if we can go all-in—even while we drive the carpool, cook dinner, order new filters for the furnace, pay the water bill, clean out the garage, and jot down the grocery list on the back of our gas station receipt—*then* we will be able to look back on these years with fondness and satisfaction.

I've learned a thing or two since becoming a parent, and one of the most important is this: success in parenting my kids means showing up and giving my best to what matters most right now. Which means, of course, that I have to *know* what matters most right now.

• • • • • •

Success in parenting my kids means showing up and giving my best to what matters most right now. Which means, of course, that I have to *know* what matters most right now.

PODO HELMER VS. CHARLIE BROWN'S TEACHER

My kids were grating on my nerves. It was below zero outside, so I could hardly shuttle them all outdoors. A zoo trip was out of the question. The three-year-old had an ear infection, the newly-mobile twins were in the habit of emptying the kitchen cupboards every time I turned around, and we had just returned from a visit with family on the other side of the state. Bloated suitcases lay strewn across the living room. The fridge was nearly empty, as was my reservoir of patience. The entire day had been a battle to persuade the older kids to cooperate, keep the twins from driving me up the wall with their open-and-dump antics, and get the three-year-old's fever down until I could take her to the doctor.

You understand, then, that when the older girls ran downstairs and complained that their nine-year-old brother had been sneaking into their bedroom and hiding in the closet yet *again*, I was absolutely certain I was going to lose it.

Exasperated, I slapped down the stack of mail I had been sorting onto the cluttered mess of the countertop. As I did, our most recent read-aloud caught my eye—*On the Edge of the Dark Sea of Darkness,* the first book of the Wingfeather Saga by Andrew Peterson. I stared at it for a moment, an idea rapidly taking shape in my mind.

"Mom!" Audrey stood before me, hands on hips. "Seriously. Tell him he HAS to stop sneaking into our ROOM!"

Nine-year-old Drew whooshed around the corner, but came to an abrupt stop when he saw my displeased expression.

"Drew," I said, using the words that had formed in my mind only a moment before, "Don't be a *thwap.*"

A momentary silence filled the room. Then, fits of laughter erupted. Even the girls, irate only moments before, relaxed their shoulders and chuckled. With those four simple words, we were transported to a cottage above the cliffs of Aerwiar, watching Podo Helmer chase the pesky, mischievous *thwaps* from sneaking around his garden.

So often in parenting, I picture myself as Charlie Brown's teacher. I'm convinced my kids hear *wah wah wah wah wah wah wah* when I'm chiding, instructing, or reminding them of something I've told them umpteen times before.

"How many times have I told you?!"
"Let me explain this one more time . . ."
"Are you even LISTENING to me?"

I could have tossed out any of those reactions, and if I'm being completely honest, I'll admit that I usually do. But the response I get when I launch into the same old, same old is the same old, same old glazed-over stare.

Wah wah wah wah wah wah wah.

Instead, this moment—born out of nothing more than

exhaustion and a quick glimpse at the cover of the book we'd recently been reading together—allowed us a paradigm shift. No lecture or further explanation was necessary. Drew knew exactly what I meant by, "Don't be a thwap."

Keep out of places you don't belong.

Don't be a pest.

Don't be a sneak.

Any of those commands would have done the trick, but none nearly so well—and certainly none as effective at lightening the mood and giving us all a much-needed chuckle.

That time, the story won the day. It broke through the monotony and the frustration. It gave us our own inside joke. Suddenly, life felt lighter. Even in the midst of conflict, we felt more connected to each other than we had been only a few moments before.

Score: Podo Helmer: 1, Charlie Brown's Teacher: 0.

TO BE ASTONISHED

Most days I am overwhelmed by the demands of raising a family. There are endless tasks—laundry, dinner, doctor appointments, sibling squabbles. I'm disciplining, cleaning, organizing, planning, listening, and doling out advice, instructions, and reminders. When the days are long and my energy (not to mention my patience) is running low, I don't have a lot of extra to give.

But isn't extra what I need? Extra—so I can make those meaningful and lasting connections with my kids that will stand the test of time. Extra—so that I can lean over and notice the ant skittering across the sidewalk.

It is on days like these when the power of reading aloud really shines. It requires so very little of me other than sitting down and reading words on a page. The book does the work for me.

Whether we are visiting Podo's garden in Aerwiar, a snowy hovel in Narnia, or Ramona Quimby's cellar on Klickitat Street, a little spark is lit. We all know it only takes a spark to start a wildfire. When my heart longs to connect with my kids but my energy reserves are depleted, a spark is exactly what I need.

In our house, whenever anyone says the word *fascinating*, someone else will interject (in the nerdiest voice they can muster), "Fascinating! Simply *fascinating!*" This comes from Kate DiCamillo's hilarious Mercy Watson series, and every time it happens, it catches us a little off guard and makes everyone laugh. It's a single word that triggers a family joke. I hope when my kids are grown, they'll hear the word *fascinating* and that fond memory will rise to the surface to warm them, wherever they may be.

If you're visiting my house, and you need something to write with, you can ask for a pen, but you may as well ask for a *frindle*. I've done this countless times during tense moments of helping a child with a difficult school assignment, and it never fails to draw out a delightful smirk from my kids. You would smirk, too, if you had read about Nick Allen causing a ruckus (and driving one of his teachers up the wall) in Andrew Clements's middle-grade novel, *Frindle*.

And when one of my young children hollers from their bed, needing one more drink of water or one more snuggle, I quietly recite a page from Anna Dewdney's *Llama Llama Red Pajama*: "Little Llama don't you know Mama Llama loves you so? Mama Llama's always near, even if she's not right here." And they remember, without my saying it, that when they have a hard time falling asleep, everything is just fine—even in the dark.

The stories we read together act as a bridge when we can't seem to find another way to connect. They are our currency, our language, our family culture. The words and stories we share become a part of our family identity.

This is exactly what happened in the family of Clay and Sally Clarkson. Clay and Sally have dedicated their lives to encouraging and equipping Christian parents to raise God-loving kids through their nonprofit organization, Whole Heart Ministries. They have written several books about how they raised their four children in a home filled with stories and read-alouds. Now, those four kids are all grown and have moved on to their own lives.

"We were all together for Christmas recently," the Clarksons' oldest daughter Sarah said, "and the number of references to stories . . . it's just a part of the way we speak about life with each other. We share stories. It's what we do. Those stories created a deep friendship between us."[1]

Of all the things I want most for my children, true friendship with one another is one of my greatest desires. Sibling arguments can be a painful and tiring experience for everyone involved—and they can make a mother in the thick of parenting wonder if her children will *ever* learn to get along.

My prayer is that despite the inevitable sibling squabbles, my kids will share so many good memories that they'll look back on their childhood and see that it was full of notice-the-ant moments. Full of thwaps and laughter and little memories they shared with each other as they first discovered Aerwiar, first climbed through the wardrobe to Narnia, took the first bite of every apple in Ramona Quimby's cellar.

I hope that some of their best memories will be the times we were astonished at what we saw, what we read, and who we met. Astonished at the magic we experienced. Astonished at the big, beautiful world and the amazing people we share it with.

Astonished.

STORIES ARE COMFORT FOOD

Courtney, a *Read-Aloud Revival* podcast listener, wrote to me about a particularly hard time in her family. Her husband had been out of work, and the financial stress was putting a gray cloud over the family. *When would he find work? How much longer could they get by? How could they deal with the stress?*

Financial strain, of course, takes its toll not only on the parents in a family but also on the children. Courtney and her husband both noticed that the longer he was out of work, the worse the children's behavior continued to get.

"I remember one night, specifically, when the kids were just at each other's throats," Courtney said. "I decided to remove my little guy from the situation and read him a book. We read one book . . . then another . . . then another. With each book, another one of my children would join us on the couch until my lap was full.

"I cannot remember a time when we felt as connected as a family as we did in that exact moment. It was as if all the stressors of life had just vanished, and we could be *us* again. It was a moment I'll never forget."

Author Tsh Oxenreider of TheArtofSimple.com and *The Simple Show* podcast recently spent nine months traveling the world with her husband and three young kids. From China to Singapore to Australia, Uganda, France, Croatia, and beyond, they trekked for nearly a year, gaining a unique and rich travel experience. She recounted the adventure in her memoir, *At Home in the World*. This wasn't their first time traveling internationally with their children, and before they left for this particular trip, Tsh said that even as they trek through new countries and continents around the globe, they still make time to read together. Why?

"When we're in a new city," Tsh said, "we've done nothing but meet new people, eat new foods, have new experiences. And yet at the end of the day, whether in a hotel room or a tent or even on a plane, we can open up *If You Give a Moose a Muffin* or *Blueberries for Sal* or some other book we've read a hundred times, and it's comfort food. It reminds us *this is who we are.*"[2]

Stories are comfort food. Stories are inside jokes. Stories are ant moments. They bond us together even when life is hard. When we pull a child onto our lap and break open the pages of a book, we're taking them by the hand and walking them into a quiet garden in the center of a noisy, polluted city. We are enveloped by the respite, just for a few moments. We are grateful for one another's company in the garden. And we rise out of the heat of a hard day and seek something better for each other.

ENEMY AMONG US

It had been a wonderful retreat—a weekend filled with twinkle lights, uplifting music, new and deepened friendships, and inspiring speakers. When it ended, four hundred moms returned home to their families. I went home to Washington state, and Stacey, a *Read-Aloud Revival* podcast listener, returned to her family in Tennessee.

Only a month later, Stacey's family learned that the symptoms her five-year-old daughter had been experiencing were evidence of an enemy in their midst. The diagnosis: leukemia.

Stacey's entire family was shocked.

"I found myself reaching for a book and reading aloud when I didn't know what else to do," Stacey said, recounting hospital stays, endless rounds of blood work, medicine, pain, suffering, and overwhelming worry.

"I think [read-alouds have] always been a grounding tool for us, though I didn't fully realize it before," she said. "We'd all get such a sense of peace when we were reading together. It helped us through the hardest parts."

I know one thing from Courtney's experience of reading aloud while her family struggled through financial difficulties and from Stacey's experience as they fought back the onslaught of childhood cancer. Their children may not remember the exact stories, plot lines, or characters of the books they shared during these times. Whether they remember the titles of the books they read together doesn't even really matter. But I am certain of one thing: they will not forget that their mama read to them.

They won't forget how the hardest times of their childhood were eased by the sharing of stories, by the opportunity to leave the noisy, polluted city of life and stand for a time in the quiet of the garden with the people they love most of all.

I've heard from countless parents that reading aloud has helped their families through the hardships of adoption, illness, emotional struggle, loneliness, and painful separation. When we read with our kids, we step outside the noise, the hustle, the friction, and for just a few minutes, we are completely and totally present with them. That simple act can make even the hardest, most painful season of life just a bit sweeter.

Lara, another *Read-Aloud Revival* podcast listener, wrote to me about how her family struggled when her husband deployed. Lara was homeschooling and trying to keep up with laundry, housework, meal prep, and vision and speech therapy sessions for the kids, along with all the other endless tasks associated with raising a family.

"I was pouring so much of myself out to my children," she wrote, "but I was still feeling so disconnected from them. There was no lasting joy. I longed for something more in my relationship with my kids."

Lara stumbled across the *Read-Aloud Revival* podcast and binge listened. She began to read with her kids more intentionally and frequently, and she found that reading aloud was about the only time she wasn't stressed. "It became my happy place through those grueling months with [my husband] gone," she said. "[Reading aloud] literally saved my relationship with my children. It gave me hope that I could still connect with them even after hard days of constant discipline. All I had to do was read the words on the page.

• • • • • •

When we read with our kids, we step outside the noise, the hustle, the friction, and for just a few minutes, we are completely and totally present with them.

"My kids don't even know how much I love reading to them," she said happily. "They think they are the ones getting the better end of the deal. In my head, I'm just thinking: mission accomplished."

MISSION ACCOMPLISHED

On that overcast spring day at the zoo so many years ago, I became acutely aware that the small, seemingly inconsequential moments in life are the ones that matter most of all. I also realized they were the ones I'd miss if I wasn't paying attention.

Those little moments, lined up one after another like beads on a string, add up to a lifetime of shared experiences, moments, and memories. They're sustaining and strengthening Courtney, Stacey, Lara, and the legions of families who are enduring hard times. They are, in the end, the moments that matter most.

Reading aloud, as simple and quiet and insignificant as it

may seem, is a way for us to pause, enjoy, and delight in *these kids*, in *this day*, in *this ant* skittering across *this path*. These moments will live on in our children's hearts even when our kids no longer live in our homes.

● ● ● ●

These moments will live on in our children's hearts even when our kids no longer live in our homes.

So I ask myself today: Why do I seem determined to wait on a walrus when so many ant moments are here for the taking? Can I make a small and lasting memory with my kids today by picking up a book of fairy tales and reading one aloud? Someday, I hope my children are wandering in a bookshop or picking through a garage sale and see the cover of a book of fairy tales. And when they do, I pray that they will remember who they are, where they came from, and to Whom they belong.

I read aloud to my kids because I know that my years with them are short. Because I long for a deep, soulful, real connection with each of them. And because I hardly want to spend these precious years waiting for the walrus, missing every ant moment while I wait. When my head hits the pillow each night, I want to know that I have done the one most important thing: I have fostered warm, happy memories and created lifelong bonds with my kids—even when the rest of life feels hard.

● ● ● ●

I read aloud to my kids because I know that my years with them are short.

These are moments we will never regret. Even better, these are moments our kids will treasure for the rest of their lives.

Chapter 3

ROAR OF THE LION

Inspiring Heroic Virtue

• • • •

> Aslan threw up his shaggy head, opened his mouth, and uttered a long, single note; not very loud, but full of power. Polly's heart jumped in her body when she heard it. She felt sure that it was a call, and that anyone who heard that call would want to obey it and (what's more) would be able to obey it, however many words and ages lay between.
>
> C. S. Lewis, *The Magician's Nephew*

Drew was four when he first heard the story of George Washington and the cherry tree. I hoisted him, sweaty and smelling of earth and grass, onto my lap one summer morning and read aloud the legend of when young George Washington received a hatchet at only six years old.

The story goes that in his youthful foolishness, George used the hatchet on one of his father's prized cherry trees. He immediately regretted his rash decision, knowing that a whipping was likely coming his way as punishment for carelessly destroying his father's property. When his father approached him about it, the boy drew himself up and proclaimed with bold honesty, "I cannot tell a lie; I did cut it with my hatchet." Surprisingly, George did not get in trouble for his actions. In legendary wisdom, his father declared that an honest son was worth more than a thousand cherry trees.[1]

Drew listened intently while I read the story, then ran out to the backyard to play with his sisters.

Later that afternoon, while scrubbing the overflowing stack of dishes from the previous night's spaghetti dinner, I looked through the window above the kitchen sink just in time to notice Drew hacking at my yellow tea roses with a large stick, his little body swinging from side to side in exuberant destruction.

I threw the dishrag to the floor, flung open the sliding glass door, and shrieked for him to stop, demanding he tell me just *what* on earth he was doing. He dropped his stick and turned glittering brown eyes toward me as a wide smile spread across his face.

"Ask me if I did it!" he exclaimed, proudly pointing at the drooping rosebush.

And then I knew.

I sank wearily onto the back step. "Did you . . . beat down . . . my tea roses?" I asked weakly.

He scrunched up his face and puffed out his chest. "I cannot tell a lie!"

THE GIFT OF PRACTICE

A story allows our children to practice living through an experience vicariously. We can't stand next to our children through every hardship they encounter, and we can't shoulder every burden. As Anne Lamott noted in her 2017 TED Talk, "12 Things I Know for Sure,"[2] we can't chase after our children with sunscreen and Chapstick into their adult years. As they grow and move out into the world, they'll face struggles in work, relationships, and all manner of situations. We can't bear the brunt of it all for them, and we don't really want to, anyway. We want our children to be brave, kind, and honest—and how will that be possible if they've never had the opportunity to face fear, unkindness, and the temptation to do wrong?

Realizing we can't protect our children from the worst parts of the world—it's almost too much to bear for those of us who love our children desperately, isn't it? Our hearts ache, knowing we can't protect our kids from everything. In fact, we can't protect them from *anything* once they have left our homes.

However, we *can* give them something that will help them. We can offer them something even better than protection. We can give them practice—lots and lots of practice.

Our modern kids don't often have opportunities to be particularly brave, much less perform heroic acts as children. But a child who has been there with Rudi as he struggles to the top of the Citadel in *Banner in the Sky*; has defied odds to prove up her late uncle's claim all on her own with *Hattie Big Sky*; has romped through the Ozarks with Billy, Old Dan, and Little Ann in *Where the Red Fern Grows*—that child has lived vicariously through the pages of a book. A child who has heard these stories will have been given practice that will prepare her in a way ordinary childhood could not possibly offer.

If a child has read widely, he'll have seen more than he ever would have living in a suburban American town, exploring the streets of a big city, or picking his way through a country field. He'll have lived through all of that, and more. He'll have travelled the world and spread lupine seeds over hillsides to make the world the more beautiful with *Miss Rumphius*; tricked the big bad wolf by audaciously rolling down the hill in a butter churn as in Paul Galdone's account of *The Three Little Pigs*. He'll have braved a swirling snowstorm and faced his foes along with *Brave Irene* and climbed the ladder to gather the secret ingredient (and discovered courage he didn't know he had) with Grandma in *Thundercake*.

Teens reading books like the youth adaptation of *The Boys in the Boat* or Corrie ten Boom's *The Hiding Place* will discover true accounts of tremendous heroism. Younger children—even the very youngest hearing fairy tales and fables—face odds and overcome struggles right alongside their favorite characters. Fiction and nonfiction stories provide children of all ages an opportunity to experience what it feels like to be overwhelmed, struggle, fight, overcome, and emerge a hero.

"To be brave in whatever situations you encounter—to be someone who can be kind . . . you've lived those hard decisions in your imagination, which is really almost as good as experiencing it yourself," children's book author Carolyn Leiloglou said on an episode of the Read-Aloud Revival podcast.[3]

When we read aloud, we give our kids practice living as heroes. Practice dealing with life-and-death situations, practice living with virtue, practice *failing* at virtue. As the characters in our favorite books struggle through hardship, we struggle with them. We consider whether we would be as brave, as bold, as fully human as our favorite heroes. And then we grasp—on a deeper, more meaningful level—the story we are living ourselves as well as the kind of character we will become as that story unfolds.

When we read *The Long Winter*, we vicariously suffer through long, meager, lonely times and start to understand the true meaning of gratitude. When we read *The Lion, the Witch and the Wardrobe*, we consider whether we would make the same decision Edmund made to follow the White Witch. When we read

Anne of Green Gables, we try on the emotions of impulsivity, imagination, and loneliness, and we experience the depths of despair. When we read *Peter Nimble and His Fantastic Eyes*, we get a glimpse of what it might feel like to be unable to see, living in a new place surrounded by people we don't know and charged with a great task.

"As the character's struggles become our own," Jamie Martin writes in *Give Your Child the World*, "we root for good to win, and we grasp more deeply the story we are writing with our own lives. A powerful story quickens the hero's heartbeat within us. Well-chosen words touch and transform our souls—making us want to become better than we are right now."[4]

As parents, there is so much we need to teach our children. There are lessons to impart—wisdom and insight to offer before our kids launch into the world on their own. But a didactic lesson or reprimand from Mom or Dad will only go so far. There is simply no substitute for story. When it comes to imparting truth to our kids, nagging lectures from an adult simply can't compare with a story whose time has come. A story meets the child where he is. It sparks an authentic desire within him to do better, try harder, and love more. It allows each of our kids a vicarious experience, giving them the precious gift of practice. Stories reach us where nothing else can and quicken the heartbeat of the hero within us.

· · · ·

There is simply no substitute for story.

QUICKENING THE HEARTBEAT OF A HERO

I want my children to know this: Courage is not the absence of fear, but rather it is the boldness to act rightly even in the face of fear. I can sit my six children down and verbally explain this. I can write a definition of the word *courage* on the board, illustrating that the word comes from the Latin root *cor* which means "heart," and therefore means to take heart and behave with spirit and pluck when the odds are against you. I can brainstorm with my children ways to demonstrate courage in everyday life. I can suggest they introduce themselves to the new family down the street or stand up for a kid at the park who is getting picked on. I can implore them to show courage when facing a needle at the doctor or a drill at the dentist. That takes courage of some sort, but not the kind that quickens the hero's heartbeat within me—and I'm absolutely certain it wouldn't quicken the hero's heartbeat within my kids.

The problem, of course, is that it's a boring and uninspiring lesson. I'm stifling a snore just thinking about it. I don't want my greatest act of heroism to be overcoming shyness or having a cavity filled. I was made for more than that. And my kids? They were, too.

What if, instead of sitting my children down to the didactic lesson above, I cuddled with them on the couch and began reading the Wingfeather Saga? We'd join the Igiby children in facing the fearsome Fangs of Dang, reaching deep within themselves to find what they need to live as crown jewels of Anniera, facing insurmountable odds with a tenacity they didn't know they had. We'd lose ourselves in the story and witness firsthand what it looks like to be truly courageous. We'd see that, in no uncertain terms, there can be no courage when there is no adversity, no virtue in staying without the temptation to run away. There can be no honor when there is no opportunity for sin.

The courage of a hero starts to beat dimly, slowly, quietly within our hearts, growing steadier and steadier as we walk through the story with Janner and Tink and Leeli, as we vicariously live as chosen ones called to a harder and higher path.

I once heard Andrew Peterson, author of the Wingfeather

Saga say, "If you want a child to know the truth, tell him the truth. If you want a child to love the truth, tell him a story."

We don't want our kids to grow up and face adversity, asking themselves, "Do I have what it takes?" We want them to *know*. We want them to have witnessed so many heroes living with integrity and fighting against their own weaknesses that they trust in the sureness of doing the right thing, even when no one is watching. We want them to stand up like warriors. Forget asking, "Do I have what it takes?" We want them to ask, "What kind of hero will I become?"

> • • • • •
>
> "If you want a child to know the truth, tell him the truth. If you want a child to love the truth, tell him a story."

When we read *Bud, Not Buddy* by Christopher Paul Curtis, my children faced the question, "What would you do if you were locked overnight in a shed like Bud was?" They had to ask themselves whether they would stay in Hooverville or hop the train. They had to wonder if they would be as brave or as positive as Bud, even in those dark and difficult days of the Great Depression. Since my children have never had to encounter the kind of cruelty, prejudice, or hardship that Bud had to overcome, those were questions that touched them in new places—that reached them in a new way.

My three oldest kids were still quite young when I first read aloud *The Wonderful Wizard of Oz* by L. Frank Baum. After reading the part where the Tinman and Scarecrow debate whether it's more important to have a heart or a brain, I decided to pose a question to my young listeners—then ages nine, seven, and five.

"Which do *you* think is more important?" I asked, "A heart? Or a brain? If you could only pick one, which would you choose?"

Audrey didn't miss a beat, answering with "brains" before I had finished asking the question.

"But how would you love God?" cried Allison, "And how would you ever fall in love?"

There began a short but powerful conversation about how important it is that we let neither the brain nor the heart override the other. When we met the Cowardly Lion, we added courage to that mix, realizing how important it is to think deeply, love fully, *and* face our fears.

I'm not sure I could have pulled off that conversation on my own if the story hadn't propelled us. I'm certain it wouldn't have sunk in as deeply as it did that day. It didn't leave an imprint only on my kids, after all—here I am, nearly seven years later, still talking about it. Clearly, it made an impact on *me* as well.

• • • •

If we tell them enough stories, they will have encountered hard questions and practiced living through so many trials, hardships, and unexpected situations that, God willing, they will have what they need to become the heroes of their own stories.

By the time our children leave our homes, we don't want them to wonder whether their lives matter. We want them to *know* that they do. If we tell them enough stories, they will have encountered hard questions and practiced living through so many trials, hardships, and unexpected situations that, God willing, they will have what they need to become the heroes of their own stories.

VEHICLES OF TRUTH

I often get wrapped up in my own little world. Frustrations and problems that arise on an ordinary day consume much of my time and energy. The skylight starts leaking, one of the twins breaks an arm (again), the power goes out for a couple of days and we lose all the meat in the freezer. It's at times like these that I lose perspective. I fall prey to it more often than I'd like to admit—the navel-gazing and myopic introspection that consumes an inappropriate amount of my time and energy. I forget that, just like Horton's speck, I am—we are—a tiny yet important part of a bigger, better story.

When I read a story with my children, though, the fog lifts, and I remember. I look up. I see it—that I am only one small part of a great, big, glorious world, and that the Maker of it exists—and has existed—always. That we are all part of his plan. That we have been invited to seek and follow him, no matter what the situation. The book becomes a set of supercharged binoculars, helping us to see beyond our normal capacity—inviting us to take part in something beyond ourselves.

A story does this on its own without our having to say a word about it. Forget the whiteboard. Forget the didactic lesson. Forget the teaching points or the comprehension worksheets. When we're telling our children the story of Jesus healing Jairus's daughter, of curing the lepers, of raising Lazarus from the dead, we don't need to wrap up the story with a trite explanation about how God is powerful, good, or merciful. We don't have to add anything at all, because there it is—truth bubbling up out of the story. It *is* the story. When God pours down manna from the heavens, a child doesn't need to be told that he will provide what we need right when we need it and not a moment before. We simply read the story, and our children feel the truth of it in their bones.

This happens with true stories that are literal accounts (such as stories within the Gospels, or historical narratives), as well as true stories that aren't meant to be literal at all (such as a myth or fairy tale). Patricia Polacco, beloved children's book author and illustrator, and recipient of many prestigious awards, told me once about her Babushka, who used to tell young Patricia and her brother all manner of tales. Brother and sister would lean forward after a story was done and whisper hopefully, "Babushka . . . is it true?" to which Babushka would exclaim with gusto, "Well, of course it's true!" and then, with a slight smile and a wink, "But it might not have happened *exactly* like that . . ."

It is this understanding that truth rises above literal facts, chronological details, or historical accountings that demonstrates how stories, especially fictional ones, have the power to speak to the hearts of readers in a profound and lasting way.

"[Story] has been the vehicle for truth for as long as the human race can remember," Newbery award-winning author Katherine Paterson wrote in a collection of essays. "Fiction allows us to do something that nothing else quite does. It allows us to enter fully into the lives of human beings."[5]

When we read a story with our children that is true—not in the literal sense, but in the supernatural sense—we don't close a book and say, "And that is how it happened, exactly like that." We say, rather, *"There he is."* Because truth always, always leads us back to gazing heavenward. Truth, whether it be factual or not, always points us back to Christ. And which is more powerful, do you think? To have an exact accounting of events in the particular order they unfolded in history, or to possess the ability to see God in every person, in every situation, in every place? To know he is omnipotent and madly in love with the world?

Realistic stories provoke our emotions and our empathy, but books that rise above facts are especially capable of helping us see the world, life, humanity, and God with startling clarity.

This is why *100 Cupboards*, the fantastically creepy and oddly inspiring middle-grade novel by N. D. Wilson, captures the attention of young readers. In this story of an ordinary boy in an ordinary town in Kansas, we discover that there is nothing mundane about where he comes from or the world in which he lives. It's an extraordinary adventure that happens in a place where nothing ever seems to happen. And what better way to enliven the imagination of a child—a child who himself feels ordinary, perhaps, than to read a tale of a boy who discovers amazing wonders right in his own humdrum surroundings? What is more electrifying to a child than to realize that he is actually living in a wild and ferocious world where big, outlandish things can happen—indeed *are* happening—all around him? An attic in Henry, Kansas seems typical until we find ourselves there with the main character of *100 Cupboards,* battling an evil witch-queen and encountering fearsome creatures from another world.

While crafting his Wilderking trilogy, Jonathan Rogers said he nearly created a swamp goblin, just to liven things up and keep things interesting. He decided not to when his wife posed the question, "Why would you have a swamp goblin when you have alligators?" Indeed, in the dreaded Feechiefen, nothing (aside from feechies, of course) is so treacherous and frightening as the swamp gators. Alligators seem ordinary to our modern minds until we hear them hissing and see them lurking in the swamp waters of the story.

"Fairy tales say that apples are golden only to refresh the forgotten moment when we found out they were green," G. K. Chesterton wrote. "They make rivers run with wine only to make us remember, for one wild moment, that they run with water."[6]

What the best stories do—and tales of fantasy do it better than anything else—is strip away the familiar in order to reveal a more prevailing, universal truth. They help us notice the breathtaking world we otherwise take for granted. They give us dragons, monsters, and witches, and then they inspire within us a knight courageous enough to slay the dragon, a hero brave enough to stand up to the monster, a heroine coy enough to sneak past the witch.

We are inspired by what is worth fighting for and what is worth dying for. We see evil for what it is; we cling to what is good. We enter into magical lands and see the body of Aslan lying dead on the cold stone table. And we feel deep within us the bold and plain truth: laying down one's life for another is the most sincere act of love. And in the end—the very, very end—good does indeed *always, always* win. Happily ever after is hardly a myth for those who believe in the promise of eternal joy in heaven.

• • • •

Happily ever after is hardly a myth for those who believe in the promise of eternal joy in heaven.

This quest for truth is tucked into every story, and when we read such stories to our children, they can't help but hear it. It's the roar of the lion, the song of Aslan, the call we were created to answer. It beats within each of us already, however faintly, and it encourages us that we have what it takes to do what is right in the face of hardship, when no one is looking and when we would rather do what is easy.

LIVE A THOUSAND LIVES

It is said that a person who reads lives a thousand lives, but a person who never reads lives only one. What better opportunity can we give our children than to live a thousand lives before they leave home? What better way to prepare them for anything they may encounter than to let them slay a thousand dragons, die a thousand deaths, live as a thousand heroes?

It turns out the story of George Washington and the cherry tree is not factual. One of Washington's biographers created the legend in the early nineteenth century. But even though it is not a literal historical accounting of young George's life, it stirred something within four-year-old Drew that helped him see himself not just as a small child in a suburban backyard, battling back a bush of tea roses, but as a hero in the making.

A childhood filled with stories that inspire and nurture the heartbeat of a hero within us is one of the simplest ways we can love and prepare our children. By doing so, we help them understand that the call to be a hero is a call to fully live God's vision for their life. We read in the hope that our children will feel the heartbeat of a hero thrumming within them and look to the heavens and ask, *What great thing have I been created to accomplish?*

C. S. Lewis says it best: "Since it is so likely that they will meet cruel enemies, let them at least have heard of brave knights and heroic courage. Otherwise you are making their destiny not brighter but darker."[7]

A well-crafted tale allows our children to see their world with fresh eyes. To notice the extraordinary wonder that it is. As we share stories with our kids, the heartbeat of a hero beats quietly within each of them. They encounter hardships and trials alongside their favorite characters. They face seemingly insurmountable odds. They draw on courage they didn't know they had.

By reading aloud with them, we help our kids understand that life will be difficult, perhaps more difficult than they can yet imagine, but that they—just like the heroes in the tales from their childhood—are capable of facing unimaginable hardship with heroic virtue. Story by story, they slowly realize that inside each of us dwells a hero.

Chapter 4

READY OR NOT

Preparing for Academic Success

• • • •

> The least expensive thing we can give a child outside of
> a hug turns out to be the most valuable: words.
>
> Jim Trelease, *The Read-Aloud Handbook*

When I was eleven, I dreamed about becoming a radio news broadcaster. My dad listened to news radio every morning in the old peach Zephyr on our way to school, and while the morning anchor's voice relayed traffic updates and local news, I imagined I was her. In my mind's eye, I was wearing a large set of important headphones, leaning over a complex audio dashboard.

"When I grow up, I'm going to do her job," I told my parents.

Apparently, they believed me. On my twelfth birthday, Dad surprised me at school. "Lunch out for your birthday!" he said with a twinkle in his eye. "Let's go to Red Robin!"

I threw my backpack into the Zephyr and climbed into the passenger seat. We listened to Paul Harvey the whole way. Talk radio filled my childhood, and I loved every minute of it.

No sooner had we sat down at the restaurant than the morning radio anchor herself scooted into the seat across from me. I knew her instantly—I would have recognized that voice anywhere.

"Happy birthday, Sarah! Mind if I join you for lunch?"

I was starstruck, but not too starstruck to engage my hero in conversation for the next hour. *What was it like to have to be at work at four in the morning? What degree did she get in college? Did she always know she wanted to be a radio newscaster?*

The anchor asked why I wanted to go into news broadcasting. I wish I could say I responded with an inspired answer. Instead, I told her that everyone said I talked a lot, so I figured I should make it my career. I remember she wasn't impressed by that answer.

It wasn't until my mid-thirties, however—after I had launched the *Read-Aloud Revival* podcast and even sometime after it had acquired its first million downloads—that I realized I had become what I'd always wanted to be, after all. I didn't broadcast on radio. I never went to school for journalism or communications. The word *podcast* didn't even exist back on that birthday when I sat chatting with my hero over cherry Cokes and a basket of bottomless fries. All the same, I now had a job talking on a podcast that aired for families all over the world. If I could have told my seventh grade self that, it would have made me downright giddy.

When you reflect back on your childhood self, does it make you wonder what will become of your own children when they are grown? I think about it all the time. Will this one still be making art when she is older? Will that one become an entrepreneur? A teacher? A florist? Have a big family? A small one? Travel the world?

I like to daydream about my children's futures because I have a hunch that I'm getting glimpses right now of what they may someday look like. Every day I get a peek into their gifts and talents—what they like to spend their time doing, what their great contributions to the world might be.

I don't think it was a coincidence that I ended up in radio. I don't think those were unrelated fanciful schemes and day-dreams. When I was just a child, God put that longing in my heart; I'm certain of it. I didn't realize it at the time, but all those years he was nurturing the seeds that would grow into what they are today—the work that fuels and satisfies me and contributes to the world.

And so I look at each of my six kids and wonder which seeds will germinate and grow into something in their own future. I have the opportunity right now, today, to prepare them for what lies ahead. I get to water the seeds. I get to encourage their wildest daydreams and give them every advantage—just like my own dad did with that surprise birthday lunch with my childhood hero—to help them bloom into the people God created them to be. What an honor! And what a responsibility!

While I'm excited about the possibilities that lie within each of my kids' futures, I'm also overwhelmed by the fact that I don't know what those futures entail, or what each of my kids will need academically in order to succeed in that work. After all, I can't predict what will come up in each of my kids' lives—which skills they'll need, which school subjects will prove most helpful in their future careers, which internal resources they'll most need to draw from in order to tackle their life's work.

When I'm speaking at a homeschooling conference, I often ask the crowd of parents to raise their hands if they are worried about teaching their children everything they need to know before their kids leave home. Without fail, nearly everyone raises their hand. Then I ask, "How many of you think it's *possible* to teach your children everything they need to know before they leave home?" The stillness of the room speaks for itself.

Forbes magazine estimates that the average adult changes

careers fifteen to twenty times over a lifetime.[1] What that means is we can't really know for sure what our kids will need down the road. Parenting is a giant act of faith for all of us. I can run myself ragged trying to give my children everything they might possibly need in their future. There are a million good experiences I can give my kids, a million worthwhile books, classes, and opportunities that could be of some benefit to their future.

But the sky is never the limit when it comes to people, is it? We are all limited by time, resources, and energy. Just like those parents who raise their hands during my speaking sessions, you and I are in the same boat. We have to push forward and make decisions about what is worth our time and what is not—about what gets our best attention, what gets our peripheral attention, and what gets no attention at all.

It makes sense, then, to consider what we can do as parents to set our kids up for academic success in general, rather than just success within a particular subject or field. There's a way to do just that, and it's easier than you might think.

• • • • •

> We have to push forward and make decisions about what is worth our time and what is not—about what gets our best attention, what gets our peripheral attention, and what gets no attention at all.

THE ART OF LEARNING TO THINK

When Dr. Catherine Pakaluk was young, she attended a small high school that was light on math and science and heavy on the liberal arts. That is, she read a lot more than she calculated. This frustrated young Catherine to no end. All through her high school years, she worried that she wasn't being prepared for the future she imagined for herself in the field of science.

She graduated and was admitted into an Ivy League school by the skin of her teeth.

"I was completely disadvantaged compared to the other kids who attended Harvard—kids who had come from schools with huge math and science programs," Catherine said. "Right away, I could see that I was learning everything from scratch. The other students had had much earlier exposure to sophisticated science and math concepts than I did."

Harvard coursework wasn't a cakewalk for anyone, of course. A couple of weeks in, all the students were essentially in the same place—equally drowning or, at best, treading water. The little advantage the other students had initially had over Catherine disappeared within about a month.

Then the tables turned. Those students who had taken AP classes in their math-and-science-focused high schools started coming to Catherine for help. She was outperforming her peers, and they wanted to know how she was doing so well with her lab reports and write-ups.

All through her high school years, Catherine had been frustrated at the vast amount of reading and literature required of her when she was convinced that a math-and-science-based education would better suit her goals. She found, however, that those years of reading literature had prepared her for higher level math and science in a unique way.

"Reading literature does this thing to your brain, to the way you think about information, which is inherently superior to mastering recipes of skills," Catherine said. "I was able to take a set of skills which I had not formerly applied to science and scientific inquiry, and succeed much more easily than my peers, who had only spent their high school years mastering scientific content."[2]

Catherine's experience helps prove that reading to our kids teaches them to think, make connections, and communicate. Reading aloud doesn't just open windows. It flings wide the doors of opportunities far outside the scope of language and literature.

It hardly seems possible that the return on investment for such a simple, basic activity can reap rewards that benefit our children in every career they'll ever have. But just so you don't have to take it from me or Dr. Catherine Pakaluk, let's look to the researchers who are digging into the data.

READING ALOUD: A MAGIC PILL

Educational experts all over the world are continually chasing after factors that could potentially produce better test scores. Smaller class sizes? Continuing education for teachers? Longer school days? Bigger budgets? There is good cause for them to seek answers, of course, but it strikes me as slightly ironic that such large sums of time, money, and energy are spent in search of what could give our generation of students an academic boost, while the power lies right in the hands of the average parent in his or her home. If you want to make sure your parental time and energy will make the biggest difference and strongest impact in your child's academic life, look no further than the closest bookshelf.

Dr. Joseph Price, associate professor of economics at Brigham Young University, specializes in the economics of family and education. His research demonstrates that one extra day per

● ● ● ● ●

If you want to make sure your parental time and energy will make the biggest difference and best impact in your child's academic life, look no further than the closest bookshelf.

week of parent-child read-aloud sessions during the first ten years of a child's life increases standardized test scores by half a standard deviation. That's as many as 15–30 percentile points—a tremendous gain.[3]

In *The Read-Aloud Handbook*, Jim Trelease suggests that the academic benefits alone of reading aloud are so great, if someone invented a pill to deliver those benefits, there would be a line for miles and miles to get it. Parents would fall over themselves and pay enormous amounts of money to give their kids the benefit of this pill. He cites the 1985 Commission on Reading that I mentioned in chapter 1: "The single most important activity for building the knowledge required for eventual success in reading is reading aloud to children."[4]

Trelease also describes the results of research conducted by the Organization for Economic Co-operation and Development, which showed that the more children are read to, the higher their test scores are—sometimes by as much as a half a year's schooling. This was true regardless of a family's income. He goes on to say that reading aloud has proven to be so powerful in increasing a child's academic success that it is more effective than expensive tutoring or even private education.

"Parents often ask me if they should play Mozart to their babies, or buy them expensive teaching toys, or prohibit television, or get them started early on a computer," Trelease writes. But the answer is much simpler: "Read to your children."[5]

This is just the tip of the iceberg when it comes to the research and data that explains the power that reading aloud has on a child's academic growth, but three benefits immediately rise to the surface to explain how reading aloud can be this effective.

THREE BENEFITS OF READING ALOUD

Benefit #1: Increased vocabulary and highly sophisticated language patterns

When it comes to prekindergarten skills, vocabulary matters more than everything else. It is, as Jim Trelease articulates in *The Read-Aloud Handbook*, "the prime predictor of school success or failure."[6]

Hearing words that don't ordinarily come up in a round of conversation expands a child's vocabulary faster and better than anything else. Kids hear words in context and can often deduce their meanings without any further explanation.

When I consider the vocabulary I use in ordinary conversation with my kids—even my teens—I realize that my word choices are far more basic than what we'd read in a book. That book doesn't have to be an Ernest Hemingway, either. A simple picture book will often use more advanced vocabulary than we'd use in a normal conversation with a neighbor or friend. Let's face it—we don't speak in grammatically correct or sophisticated language patterns. And that's what our kids need most of all when it comes to language acquisition: grammatically correct and sophisticated language patterns.

Mandie, a *Read-Aloud Revival* podcast listener, read aloud *A Christmas Carol* by Charles Dickens to her kids. Dickens's writing is sophisticated and rich, of course, and Mandie wasn't sure how much of the story her kids were picking up. A few days later, her three-year-old ran into the room crying. She was upset because her four-year-old brother had called her a "covetous old sinner" for refusing to share her toys.

That's exactly what happens when we read with our kids.

They take grammatically correct and sophisticated vocabulary in through the ear . . . and it comes flying back out of their mouths when we least expect it.

Consider this passage from the second chapter of *The Wonderful Wizard of Oz* by L. Frank Baum, a book I often recommend parents read to children as young as four or five:

> She was awaked by a shock, so sudden and severe that if Dorothy had not been lying on the soft bed she might have been hurt. As it was, the jar made her catch her breath and wonder what had happened; and Toto put his cold little nose into her face and whined dismally. Dorothy sat up and noticed that the house was not moving; nor was it dark, for the bright sunshine came in at the window, flooding the little room. She sprang from her bed and with Toto at her heels ran and opened the door. The little girl gave a cry of amazement and looked about her, her eyes growing bigger and bigger at the wonderful sights she saw.

Most of us don't talk about our pets whining "dismally" or light "flooding" into a little room (though they do, and it does). Hearing enough of this kind of language will build within our children a storehouse of good vocabulary and accurate language patterns. As they listen to stories, their vocabulary will be strengthened without effort.

Describing the frustrations writing teachers encounter when trying to improve their students' papers, Andrew Pudewa said, "You can't get out what you don't put in."[7] If a child doesn't have a large storehouse of grammatically correct and sophisticated language patterns (and a wellspring of ideas) to draw from, he said, when it's time for their own turn at communicating—writing the research paper, the lab report, the presentation, or the college admissions essay—they won't have anything of value to draw from. But fill up that storehouse, and you'll be amazed at what lives inside them.

Vocabulary is enhanced, of course, when kids read to themselves, but it's even better when they are read *to*. That's because their listening comprehension level is higher than their reading comprehension level. Children are able to listen to stories with more complex vocabulary beyond what they are capable of reading on their own. You already know this to be true, even if you haven't considered it before. A child of five or six who is just learning to read cannot pick up a copy of *A Bear Called Paddington* and start reading it. But a parent can read *A Bear Called Paddington* aloud, and the child will keep up with the story just fine.

Benefit #2: The ability to make connections (in other words, reading comprehension)

You've probably heard much ado about *reading comprehension*. Educators are always concerning themselves over making sure our kids are doing it well. Reading comprehension is just a fancy term for considering whether a student understood what they read and whether they can apply new information to their current body of knowledge.

When we read with good comprehension, we automatically consider what else is happening at the time of the story. We connect information we're encountering for the first time to other facts and ideas we've already encountered. We compare it to stories we've heard before and hold it up against our own lives. Without even intending to, we make connections—many more than we could possibly count—every time we open the pages of a book. This is, admittedly, a simplified explanation of reading comprehension, but it captures the essence of the concept.

Here is what we know: good readers generally have good reading comprehension. As they read, they try on solutions, consider problems, and connect new information with what they already know. That's because when we're reading, we're practicing the art of thinking well. We're asking questions. We're connecting ideas.

When kids are first learning to read, they aren't doing much in the way of practicing reading comprehension. All of their brain power is focused on decoding, which is why a new reader can often sound out an entire page of words and then stare at you blankly when you ask her what she just read. She isn't being obstinate—she really doesn't know. She was putting so much energy into demystifying the letters on the page that she wasn't able to spend any mental energy on comprehension.

A child who can read Cam Jansen or Nate the Great on his own is quite capable of having his imagination captured by The Chronicles of Narnia. He will delight in the wild summer adventures in *Swallows and Amazons*, light up with the opportunity to visit *Treasure Island*, and giggle hysterically at the never-ending soliloquies of Louis' father in *The Trumpet of the Swan*. He can't do any of that on his own quite yet, though. He needs someone to do the hard work of decoding text and translating rhythm and cadence in order to fire him up and help him get lost in a story.

When we do the work of decoding for our kids—when we read a book aloud and take on the work of figuring out correct rhythms, cadence, and voice for each line—the child listening gets to spend her mental energy in a different way. She enjoys the story and makes connections. This is practice at reading comprehension.

This isn't true only for beginning readers. The importance of hearing stories above our own individual reading level continues throughout the school years. This is why I often recommend that parents who want their kids to read the classics read them aloud before they are ever assigned as schoolwork. The sophisticated language patterns and complex vocabulary in classic literature are far easier to understand when someone sorts out the logistics and reads them for you. When you listen, you can expend all of your mental energy on making connections. This is undoubtedly the richer, more impactful part of reading a classic.

As a reading adult, I still prefer to get both my Dickens and my Shakespeare through audiobooks. The nuances in dialogue and meaning are so much more obvious to me when I hear a skilled narrator read them aloud.

Any teacher will tell you that reading comprehension is critical. Children need to understand what they read and apply it to what they already know. That is the art of thinking well. When we read aloud with our kids, we give them a massive leg up at learning to think well.

Benefit #3: A love for reading

In her 2015 TEDx Talk, "Why We Should All Be Reading Aloud to Children," Rebecca Bellingham told the story of Joey, a third-grade boy at the South Bronx elementary school where she taught. On this particular day, Mrs. Bellingham was reading aloud the story of *Charlotte's Web*. Joey listened with rapt attention as she read about Wilbur's close call with Mr. Arabel's ax. In his imagination, he saw the morning light shining through Wilbur's pink skin, smelled whiffs of bacon and coffee in the farmhouse kitchen, heard the noises of breakfast being prepared—bacon sizzling, coffee perking.

After she finished the chapter that day, Joey told Mrs. Bellingham that he had never enjoyed a story so much. He felt like he was right there inside the story, and that didn't usually happen to him when he read.

I remember laying my head on my desk every day after recess during the fifth grade, relishing the stories the teacher read aloud during my favorite fifteen minutes of the school day. I felt the same way Joey did—transported inside the book in a way that didn't happen when I read on my own. Why is it that reading aloud does this to us?

"A man who does not read has no advantage over the man who cannot read," Mark Twain said.[8] The same can be said for children. If we want our children to enjoy reading—if we want them to read not just because they can, but because they want to—then we must do more than merely teach our children how to decode text.

Even more important than teaching our kids the actual skill of reading is to cultivate a deep love of stories. After all, a child must love reading if he is to do it of his own volition throughout his life.

• • • • •

Even more important than teaching our kids the actual skill of reading is to cultivate a deep love of stories.

Rebecca Bellingham took the first step with her third-grade students when she read aloud *Charlotte's Web* to them. By doing so, she did the heavy lifting of decoding sounds and interpreting rhythm and vocal cues. Because she did the work, the children were free to fall in love with the *story*.

When we focus on nurturing our children's love of stories, we get both kids who *can* read as well as kids who *do*. We need our kids to fall in love with stories before they are even taught their first letters, if possible, because everything else—phonics, comprehension, analysis, even writing—comes so much more easily when a child loves books.

If you know any voracious readers (or perhaps you are one yourself), you know that reading begets reading. The more a reader reads, the more he or she wants to read. It's a beautiful thing, really—and when we recognize the tremendous impact a healthy reading life can have on the academic success of our kids, we realize that giving them the opportunity to fall in love with books ends up being an amazing academic boon. It cultivates a natural curiosity to find out *what next* or *what else*, gives them momentum to read more, and helps them encounter new ideas and make better connections.

In the case of Dr. Catherine Pakaluk, the prolific reading she did as a child aided her scientific studies at an Ivy League school. Because she learned to think deeply and make connections in her reading, she was able to apply those skills to a subject outside of language and literature. The benefits of a healthy reading life have a wide reach. When we help our children become solid, voracious readers, they develop skills that will help them in other academic areas.

Kids don't need these skills just so they will read more nonfiction, either. As we discussed in chapter 3, stories are the way the greatest truths have always been passed on, especially within the Christian tradition. *In the beginning* and *Once upon a time* are not so different from each other, it turns out. From prophecies of old to parables to the gospel stories we read from the Bible every week at church, stories are the vehicles for imparting the most important truths we know.

• • • •

Stories are the vehicles for imparting the most important truths we know.

Reading begets reading. A child who loves to read does so voraciously. This is an academic gain that can hardly be replicated in any way except by cracking open the spine of a good book and getting lost in it.

MAGIC PILL, INDEED

Who knew a bedtime story could make such an impact? When we read aloud, we give our kids a storehouse filled with excellent vocabulary and highly sophisticated language patterns. We offer them practice at making connections and thinking well. And best of all, we help them fall in love with reading—an affection that will serve them well their entire lives.

And so, while I continue to daydream and wonder about what my children will one day become and what great vision God has for each of their lives, I'll do the *one* thing I know will best prepare them for it all. It's free. It's easy. And it's the most effective way to help my kids succeed academically. I'll read aloud.

Chapter 5

WALKING A MILE

Nurturing Empathy and Compassion

• • • •

> Build your kids' lives on a story-solid foundation and you'll
> give them . . . a reservoir of compassion that spills over
> into a lifetime of love in action.
>
> Jamie C. Martin, *Give Your Child the World*

I've known about the Sudan water crisis for as long as I can remember. I've watched news blurbs on TV and skimmed articles in the newspaper about how entire villages in Africa struggle to obtain clean water for their families. It makes me so sad, striking me with a sudden sense of despair at the overwhelming problems of the world. So much hurt. So much suffering.

Even so, I was sucker-punched last year when I read Linda Sue Park's *A Long Walk to Water*, a middle-grade novel that tells the story of two Sudanese eleven-year-olds. Half of the book is set in 1985 and based on the true story of Salva, one of the lost boys of Sudan, who crossed the entire African continent by foot in search of safety. The other half tells the story of Nya, a fictional present-day girl who spends eight hours each and every day trudging through the dusty heat, thorns puncturing her feet, sun beating relentlessly on her back, as she sets out to gather two jugs of water for her family.

Every day. Two jugs.

It's a fast read, and I devoured it in two afternoons. I read while watching my small kids play in our backyard sandbox, and every few pages I'd find myself staring at my three small children—my twin boys and my little girl. My own pair of Salvas, my own little Nya. I wondered about the children in the book, considered the magnitude of the trials they faced. How did they bear it? What must it do to the human spirit to carry such a crushing load? How on earth do others like them survive such a life?

I paused from my reading and watched one of the twins pour water through a funnel, creating a rivulet on the left side of the sandbox. His eyes gleamed at his creation as his hands playfully scattered sand in piles around the banks of his new little handmade river. Water running in such abundance.

I finished the book, got up, and called over my shoulder that I was heading inside to make dinner.

As I set the book down on the kitchen counter and stared at it, I thought of Uncle's words to Salva: "One step at a time . . . one day at a time. Just today—just this day to get through."

Silently, I filled a saucepan with water, flipped on the burner, measured rice. I grabbed a large bag of carrots from the fridge, placed them on the cutting board, and stared out the window, mulling over what I'd just read.

Crocodile attacks. Violence. Hunger. Loneliness.

Hope.

The book filled me with sorrow and, at some points, fear—but it also filled me with hope. Triumph, even. It left me with the satisfying knowledge that good always triumphs over evil, even when it's hard to see. That the human spirit can be bent but not completely broken—that the hardships lived out by Salva in 1985 could indeed be redeemed.

I didn't hear Andy come in from work. Didn't notice he was there, in fact, until he dropped a kiss on my cheek and nudged me out of the way so he could wash his hands in the sink.

"Gee, what's up with you?" he asked as he picked up the knife and took over chopping vegetables.

I couldn't answer. For the life of me, I couldn't find the words. I wiped a tear from the corner of my eye, felt my throat constrict, and weakly pointed to the book sitting on the edge of the counter in our suburban American home.

The book had altered me. *One step at a time . . . one day at a time . . .*

SLIPPING INTO ANOTHER'S SHOES

A book can reach us where a news report cannot. It's not when we hear a summary on the news of what's happening in the Middle East that our heart catches fire. It's when we hear the story of one person—one man, one woman, one child. It's when we dig out the thorn in Nya's foot, journey with her for hours in the stifling African sun, experience her loneliness and her fear. It is *then* that we feel the human-to-human connection. That's when our empathy is stirred. That's when we feel fully human.

We slip on someone else's shoes for a few minutes or 121 pages, and our spirits are moved. We are never quite the same again.

That is the power of story.

Story awakens us to the beauty and the bedlam of the world around us. It arouses within us a desire for mercy and justice and truth. Story makes us fall a little more in love with the world we live in and the people God made to live here with us.

In her book *For the Children's Sake*, Susan Schaeffer Macaulay tells us that, "In literature, perhaps more than through any other art form, we are able to get into another man's shoes."[1] It's so easy for us to cast judgment on others as we read history textbooks, skim Facebook status updates, or scan news blurbs. We are bombarded with messages all day, so it's no wonder we begin to tune them out. No wonder we find ourselves desensitized, numb, choosing to avoid the gaze of the panhandler we skirt around whenever we're downtown.

• • • •

Story makes us fall a little more in love with the world we live in and the people God made to live here with us.

The antidote to that kind of indifference is to cultivate within ourselves a sincere empathy. To live vicariously through the feelings, thoughts, attitudes, and life experiences of another—someone we would otherwise never get to know. The first step is to walk a mile in someone else's shoes.

That's what transformed me on a late summer afternoon when I finished *A Long Walk to Water*. It was as if I were trekking through the African desert myself, wondering where I would find safety, longing for just a swallow of cool water. It was only by living vicariously through the story of another—of a completely made up person, in Nya's case—that woke me up to loving the real-life people in the world around me.

When my oldest daughter, Audrey, finished reading *Red Scarf Girl*, Ji-li Jiang's memoir of China's Great Proletarian Cultural Revolution under the Communist leader Mao Zedong, she came to me wide-eyed. "How did he do that?" she asked about Chairman Mao. "How was he able to successfully convince an entire nation that his evil plans were for their own good?"

What Jiang's memoir does so well—and what every story can do that a news report cannot—is help us see life from a point of view we have never considered. What might it be like to be raised under Communist power? What thoughts might niggle their way to the surface of a twelve-year-old's mind in that situation? And what might it take for her to break free from that way of thinking?

It would be nearly impossible to read a story like *Red Scarf Girl* and remain unchanged. My own daughter's appreciation for true freedom was nourished by her realization that liberty—something she has always viewed as her God-given right—is a great gift. She was roused to a new awareness that she would not have gained if she hadn't slipped into the shoes of Ji-li Jiang.

Her heart began to throb for those who have suffered under oppressive government rule. This isn't the end of the story, of course. Reading a book like *Red Scarf Girl* is just the first step. It's the eye-opening beginning.

Raising our children isn't just about getting them ready for adulthood. It isn't just about preparation for a career. It's about transforming and shaping their hearts and minds. It's about nourishing their souls, building relationships, and forging connections. It's about nurturing within them care and compassion for whomever they encounter.

It's about taking on the mind of Christ. Just as Jesus wept when Lazarus died, we too must weep with our brothers and sisters, friends and strangers, the brokenhearted and downtrodden.

VICARIOUS READING ISN'T SO VICARIOUS

Stories, it turns out, are incredible empathy builders. The process of entering into a life different from our own compels us to see the world from another point of view. This isn't just theory. Keith

Oatley, a cognitive psychologist at the University of Toronto, helped conduct a study which showed that reading fictional stories increases the reader's empathetic response to people in their real life. In fact, researchers at Carnegie Mellon University found that reading a story gives the brain similar network connections as *actually living* through an experience yourself.[2] Vicarious reading, it turns out, isn't as vicarious as we might have thought.

In the article "Mirrors, Windows, and Sliding Glass Doors," Rudine Sims Bishop explained the phenomenon that happens when we read. According to Bishop, books can function as windows "offering views of worlds that may be real or imagined, familiar or strange." Sometimes books are mirrors that "transform the human experience and reflect it back to us." At other times, they are sliding glass doors in which readers "have only to walk through in imagination to become part of whatever world has been created or recreated by the author."[3]

When we begin to see the books we share with our children in this way—as windows, mirrors, and sliding glass doors—we start to value what is otherwise unquantifiable. We want our children to know without a doubt that people are people, whether or not they look like us, talk like us, or act like us, and that every last person on this earth deserves to be loved with wild abandon because each and every one of us is made in the image and likeness of God.

When Rebekah Gonzalez was elementary-school-age, her mother, Toni, read aloud *Johnny Tremain* by Esther Forbes. Set in Boston during the events leading up to the Revolutionary War, the book tells the story of a fourteen-year-old apprentice silversmith. After Johnny's hand is disfigured and disabled, he ends up working as a horse-riding messenger for the Sons of Liberty. As her mother read the book aloud, Rebekah fell fast for Johnny, thoroughly enjoying his adventurous story of loyalty and courage.

The next summer, Rebekah attended VBS and came home each night to talk incessantly about her new best friend, Billy. Every night, she told her mother about the funny things he had said, how smart he was at Bible memory, his cool T-shirt and stylish hair, his award for Camper of the Day.

Toni wasn't able to meet Billy until the final day of VBS. When Rebekah called Billy over to introduce him to her mother, Toni received a surprise.

Billy made his way over to Rebekah and Toni, leaning heavily on his walker. It was only then that Toni realized something: Billy had cerebral palsy. During all of those conversations about her new best friend, Rebekah had never once mentioned it.

That day, Toni noticed that most of Rebekah's VBS classmates were uncomfortable in Billy's presence. When she asked her daughter about the new friendship, Rebekah credited her fictional friend Johnny Tremain, who had taught her what it might feel like to be disabled and therefore different from everyone else.

When we finish the final chapter of a book that has touched us on a deep level and we slip back into our own shoes, we are never quite the same. We're changed. We start the book in one place and leave it in quite another—more merciful, more understanding, maybe a little more compassionate than we were before. Had Rebekah's mother not read the fictional story of Johnny Tremain to her daughter, that VBS experience might have been rather different—different for Rebekah, and surely different for Billy as well.

EDUCATION IS FOR LOVE

Shannon, a *Read-Aloud Revival* podcast listener, wrote to me about reading *Little House on the Prairie* to her eight-year-old son, Ray. When Ma and Pa had to unexpectedly pack up and leave their beloved little house with nothing to show for a year's worth of hard labor, Ray interrupted Shannon mid-sentence. From the top bunk, he blurted out, "My eyes are wet." Shannon paused. Ray sounded surprised, so she decided to probe gently.

"Bud, is that because you're crying?"

"Well," he responded, ". . . a bit." The reason for those unexpected tears? Pa left the latch string out. Instead of harboring bitterness after a year of back-splitting labor building a home he would now have to abandon, Pa chose to offer his home to any weary passersby who might be in need of shelter. Ray felt—even for just one evening, just one moment—what it might be like to experience profound disappointment, weariness, and loss, and yet still show thoughtfulness for others. To be kinder than necessary, even when it is incredibly hard to do.

Shannon could not have taught her son this lesson in any better way, I'm convinced. Pa did the teaching for her, and she didn't even realize this until it had already happened. It's now lodged deeply within the bones of a boy who will grow up to know that even when it's hard, he can still be kind. Even when he's hurting, he can be thoughtful.

What better education can we offer our children than the shaping of their hearts to love others as we have been loved by God ourselves? Charlotte Mason, a nineteenth-century educator, said as much when she taught that it's not how much children know that matters—it's how much they *care*.[4] Education is put to its best use when it teaches us how to love.

It's tempting to idolize certain aspects of education. We value good grades, high test scores, elite college degrees, and lucrative careers. But our obsession keeps us from remembering what education is for. *Education is for love.*

Is the main reason we want an excellent education for our

children so they can outperform their peers? So they can rank higher, get promoted faster, become more financially successful than their colleagues and friends? Or do we want our children to become educated so they can follow the two greatest commandments: love God and love one another?

A good education, then, is not one that results in high test scores, elite college acceptances, or the ability to read Virgil in Latin or *War and Peace* without CliffsNotes. A good education teaches us—and our children—to love fully and to love well.

• • • •

What better education can we offer our children than the shaping of their hearts to love others as we have been loved by God ourselves?

"Above all," we read in 1 Peter 4:8, "love each other deeply, because love covers over a multitude of sins." As Christians, we know our prime task is to love. Jesus Christ made that abundantly clear when he said that the greatest commandment is, "Love the Lord your God with all your heart and with all your soul and with all your mind,"[5] and then followed it up with a second commandment: "Love your neighbor as yourself."[6]

Education is at its best when we use it to help our children feel another person's pain or joy. In *To Kill a Mockingbird,* Atticus Finch tells his daughter, "If you can learn a simple trick, Scout, you'll get along a lot better with all kinds of folks. You never really understand a person until you consider things from his point of view."[7]

I called up my colleague, Rea Berg, one late summer afternoon to talk about this. Rea started a publishing company, Beautiful Feet Books, in an effort to bring the best of bygone children's literature to today's readers. I value her insight into how books can nourish the hearts and minds of kids and what role that plays in their education.

On this particular afternoon, I talked to Rea as the sun set behind the Ponderosa pines in the backyard and dust motes floated in front of my bedroom window.

● ● ● ●

A good education teaches us—and our children—to love fully and to love well.

"Look," Rea said, "we don't want to create intellectual geniuses who don't have humanity, compassion, and empathy. Intellectual genius without heart is a dangerous, dangerous thing."

A good education, then, is an education of the heart.

It includes the practice of listening—for we must truly *listen* to others in order to understand them. And it is only by understanding others that we can love them the way we are called to love them.

We read *Out of the Dust* by Karen Hesse and wonder, for the first time, what it must have been like to survive Oklahoma's Dust Bowl in the 1930s. We consider life with dirt in every bit of food, settling under our eyelids, lining our beds. Or we board a ship with Hà, the main character in Thanhha Lai's *Inside Out and Back Again*. We become her companion after the Fall of Saigon and see America for the first time through the eyes of a frightened refugee. We sleep under a bridge on the River Seine with Suzy, Paul, and Evelyne in Natalie Savage Carlson's *The Family Under the Bridge*. We learn what it means to be homeless, hungry, and in need. We experience the Danish resistance through the eyes of ten-year-old Annemarie in *Number the Stars*. We tremble with fear at the horror of the Nazi occupation and swell with compassion for those who were forced to hide or flee. We go to school with August Pullman in *Wonder* by R. J. Palacio, and we find out what it feels like to be disfigured and dismissed by peers. To be shunned.

Empathy, of course, is only the beginning. We must put legs

on that empathy in order for it to become compassion. We must turn our grief and sadness into love in action. Stories help us take that first step with our kids. As Rea said, they help us "identify with the trials, tragedies, and triumphs of others, which is the beginning of empathy."

Rea told me about a summer evening when she stood in the kitchen, preparing dinner. Her normally stoic and undemonstrative fifteen-year-old son entered the room with tears streaming down his face. He had just finished reading *Let the Circle Be Unbroken* by Mildred Taylor, and he asked his mother, "How can people treat others that way?" It was a burning cry, Rea said, for all victims and innocent bystanders of injustice throughout the ages. It was the beginning of empathy.

We read with our children because it gives both them and us an education of the heart *and* mind. Of intellect and empathy. We read together and learn because stories teach us how to love.

SALT AND LIGHT

It was almost Valentine's Day, and the Case family (*Read-Aloud Revival* podcast listeners) had stumbled across one of my own favorite picture books at the library, *Somebody Loves You, Mr. Hatch* by Eileen Spinelli.

The story is about a lonely neighborhood man who never smiles or speaks to anyone, until one day when he receives an unidentified note in the mail. The note reads simply: *Somebody loves you*. Because of the note, Mr. Hatch's whole demeanor changes. He becomes joyful and engaging, a man eager to help his neighbors and show kindness even in the smallest ways. The Case boys loved the book and asked for it to be read to them over and over again.

"Every time we read the book," the boys' mother said, "my boys and I would talk about how the simple act of speaking life into someone's world—either through a simple note or a kind gesture—can impact an individual in a big way."

Her six-year-old decided he wanted to make some notes reading *Somebody loves you* to leave in places around their community. They left them in library books, on vending machines and bathroom mirrors, on park benches, and in grocery store aisles.

Reading one simple picture book inspired the Case family to make the world a little better. The story sparked the heart of the children who read it—and the parent who read it with them.

It's astonishing how the simple act of reading with our children can so thoroughly affect them (and us), isn't it? I suspect that for most of us, reaching our kids in this way—at the core of their souls, where they feel and love most deeply—matters more to us than almost anything else.

I want so very much for my children to grow up to be kinder than necessary. I want them to love abundantly. To care for others, even when it's hard to understand them. I want them to be salt and light.

Remember my experience after reading Linda Sue Park's *A Long Walk to Water*? I am not, of course, the only one who was impacted greatly by this story. One *Read-Aloud Revival* podcast listener wrote to tell about her own experience reading the book with her kids.

"By the end of the book," she said, "I was crying my eyes out, but the kids were in love with it." The following month, her ten-year-old son told her that he and his siblings had saved up their allowance to help pay for a well.

Could those children possibly have been moved in such a profound way by a news clip, a textbook, a Facebook post, or a commercial?

As author Linda Sue Park told me, a book can't change the world on its own, but a book can change readers.[8] And readers? They can change the world. Our young readers—yours and mine—can love with abandon, show unexplainable kindness, build wells in impoverished communities, offer an unexpected smile, shake the hand of a person they'd rather avoid, or give a hug to someone who is experiencing hardship.

Our young readers can grow up to love the heck out of this world because the stories we read aloud to them during their childhood introduced them to a cast of characters wider than they could have met in any other way. Those stories can unleash unstoppable hope and compassion.

The stories offer us a beginning—a first step on the road to living a life of love. *A Long Walk to Water* left a lasting impact on me. *Red Scarf Girl* made a lasting impression on my daughter. When we read about characters—both factual and fictional—experiencing hardship and meeting injustice, something moves within us. That something is empathy—the beginning of compassion. It is a tremendous gift we give to our children every time we crack the pages of a book.

●●●●

A book can't change the world on its own. But a book can change readers. And readers? They can change the world.

PART 2

Connecting with Our Kids Through Books

Chapter 6

CREATE A BOOK CLUB
CULTURE AT HOME

• • • •

When she was hardly more than a girl, Miss Minnie had
gone away to a teacher's college and prepared herself to
teach by learning many cunning methods that she never
afterward used. For Miss Minnie loved children and she
loved books, and she taught merely by introducing the
one to the other.

Wendell Berry, *Watch with Me*

The woman plunked down a stack of magazines on the front
desk of the library where I worked and turned to her ten-year-old
daughter. "What did you find?" she asked.

The girl tucked a strand of long, sandy hair behind her ear.
"Not much, but I found this." She timidly pushed a faded paperback with a yellow-and-blue cover toward her mother.

"*The Penderwicks*!" I exclaimed from behind the checkout,
pulling the stack of magazines toward me and typing my password into the computer. "You'll love it." I picked up the book to
start scanning barcodes.

"Wait. What is that?" The girl's mother took the book from my hand and peered through her glasses, eyeing it skeptically. She turned to her daughter. "Is this on the list for school?"

"Well, no . . ." The girl started to fidget, a slight shade of pink creeping up her neck.

"You're going to waste your time reading something that doesn't even *count*?"

I bit the insides of my cheeks and watched the mother scornfully shake her head. She turned to me.

"You can put this back for us, right?" she said, tossing the book on the counter and rolling her eyes. "We'll be back in a minute. First we need to find something that's actually *on* the list." She scooped the stack of magazines back into her arms, and mother and daughter started to walk away, the mother still talking.

"Seriously, Emma, there's no use reading something that doesn't count . . ."

Seeing Emma's wistful glance toward *The Penderwicks*, now abandoned at my elbow, I bit my cheeks harder. I was struggling not to throw something at the wall.

SCHOOLING IT OUT

That particular evening, I became convinced of something I had long suspected: a sense of duty is killing our kids' ability to read for pleasure.

Jim Trelease doesn't mince words about this in *The Read-Aloud Handbook*. "Every child begins school wanting to learn to read," he writes. "In other words, we've got 100 percent enthusiasm and desire when they start school."[1]

That number declines steadily, however, beginning in late elementary school, and continues to decline rapidly every year thereafter. A typical high school student reads for pleasure approximately six minutes per day. Dr. Daniel Willingham tells us what this means in his book, *Raising Kids Who Read*. As a professor of psychology at the University of Virginia, he has researched and written about strategies to help parents enjoy books with their kids. In *Raising Kids Who Read*, he notes that those six minutes a day actually indicate that most kids don't read at all, while a very few read quite a lot.[2]

The natural question is, *why?* Trelease answers that in chapter 1 of his book: "It was either never planted or driven out by seat work and test prep, leaving no room for a pleasure connection."[3] He names the decreasing amount of time adults spend reading with kids as they get older as a major factor in the loss of the pleasure connection. Most of us stop reading to our kids as soon as they can read for themselves, and almost no one is reading aloud to middle-school and high-school age kids—parents *or* teachers. This, according to Trelease, is the main reason most kids don't read for pleasure.

It makes sense, doesn't it? Small children love the warmth and connection of sitting on Mom or Dad's lap for a story. For small kids, books equal pleasure. By middle school, though, our kids have absorbed the message that reading is something we do for a purpose—book reports, essays, or quizzes. Reading is something to get through, check off, finish already. Reading is *work*.

That day at the library, Emma's mother made it clear to her daughter that the purpose of reading is academic. Now, you and I might not say that in so many words. But my fear is that, even if we don't believe it's true, we communicate it with both our actions and expectations. I wonder if schools, teachers, and—worst of all—parents are sending a message to our kids that we read solely in order to succeed in school.

We do it without realizing it, and we do it with the best intentions. We want our children to succeed academically and demonstrate the ability to read with ease and skill. But good intentions can end in disaster. You could light a fire to stay warm, but that fire, untended, could burn down a house or a field. That fire could burn down an entire forest.

We light a fire for our smallest children, pulling them onto our laps, reading rollicking tales and delightful fables, turning pages in brightly colored picture books, getting lost in tales of *Strega Nona*, *The Little Red Hen*, *Sheep in a Jeep*. But something changes as they grow. They learn to read on their own, so we assume they don't want us to read aloud to them anymore. Their reading assignments aren't the rollicking, delightful tales of their childhood, but school assignments instead. Calendars fill, to-do lists grow, and reading for pleasure becomes a thing of the past. A memory. We slowly but surely teach our kids that reading is something you do out of duty rather than for pleasure.

"Why are we so determined to teach our children to read?" Katherine Paterson asks in her collection of essays, *A Sense of Wonder*. "So that they can read road signs? Of course. Make out a job application? Of course. Figure out the destination of the bus so that they can get to work? Yes, of course. But don't we want far more for them than the ability to decode? Don't we want for them the life and growth and refreshment that only the full richness of our language can give? . . . What good are straight teeth and trumpet lessons to a person who cannot see the grandeur that the world is charged with?"[4]

This is, perhaps, one of the most important chapters in this book, because it reminds us that reading is first and foremost for pleasure—for delight. We communicate what we believe about books by the reading atmosphere (or lack thereof) in our homes. Either we create a space where reading is something that is done for the joy of it, where the imagination is cultivated and allowed to wander and stretch and grow, or we deaden our children's natural love for the written word.

Either way, it's up to us—you and me, parents of the next generation. "If you want to raise a reader, you should not rely much on your child's school," Dr. Daniel Willingham writes in *Raising Kids Who Read*. "It's up to parents to create an atmosphere where a child's reading life can flourish."[5]

• • • • • •

Either we create a space where reading is something that is done for the joy of it, where the imagination is cultivated and allowed to wander and stretch and grow, or we deaden our children's natural love for the written word.

THE SUPREME IMPORTANCE OF DELIGHT

Here is something that may surprise you: parents who think the primary importance of reading is to be successful in school are less likely to have kids who enjoy reading than parents who see reading primarily as a venue for entertainment.

Did you catch that?

Kids whose parents believe reading is first and foremost a mode of entertainment and enjoyment end up being more voracious readers than those who want their kids to read so that they can succeed in school. They also end up being *better* readers. Our attitude about reading and the atmosphere we create in our home matter. Our kids pick up on it—even if we never say anything out loud, even if we aren't the mother at the library checkout insisting our child put back that copy of *The Penderwicks*.

It is essential that we communicate with our words, actions, and attitudes that reading is worthwhile for its own sake. Not because it improves us or helps us academically. Not because it helps us become more articulate, score better on college entrance exams, or gives us a cultural understanding of those around us. It does all those things, to be sure, but it is of paramount importance to communicate to our children that reading is pleasurable and worthwhile for the sheer delight of it. We want our kids to, as the distinguished professor of the humanities in the Honors Program at Baylor University says, "read at whim." Jacobs explains reading at whim in his insightful book, *The Pleasures of Reading in an Age of Distraction*, a commentary on the importance of reading for the sheer delight of it.

"For heaven's sake," Jacobs writes, "don't turn reading into the intellectual equivalent of eating organic greens or (shifting the metaphor slightly) some fearfully disciplined appointment with an elliptical trainer of the mind in which we count words or pages the way some people fix their attention on the 'calories burned' readout . . . how depressing."[6]

Rather, he tells us, "Read what gives you delight."[7]

Reading at whim—that is, reading for the sheer delight of it, may have a bigger impact on the life of your child than you expect. For many of us, the books we choose to read on our own are the ones that stick with us. It turns out there is nothing magical about a book once it makes it to a grade-level approved list or lands on a teacher's syllabus. The act of picking up a book and reading it for no other reason than enjoyment can open the door for significant impact.

• • • •

The act of picking up a book and reading it for no other reason than enjoyment can open the door for significant impact.

WELCOME TO BOOK CLUB

Humor me for just a moment here. Imagine you have just arrived at your book club gathering. You've spent a long day with the kids, and you're looking forward to attending this book club for the first time. This month's selection is Anthony Doerr's *All the Light We Cannot See*. The book left you speechless, and you're ready for a meaty discussion with the other members.

You are greeted at the door by the hostess, a friend who embraces you in a hug and then promptly hands you a sheet of multiple choice questions about the book. "Welcome to book club!" she says cheerily. "Go ahead and start with this. We just want to make sure you've read and understood the book before we get any further."

You take the quiz, making guesses at the city names, numbers, details, and dates. (Was the girl who haunted Werner's conscience Viennese or Parisian? Werner was . . . sixteen? Or was he seventeen? Did Madam Manec get the flu, or was it pneumonia? Did the story begin in 1944? Or was it 1934? Or somewhere in between?) You fill out the answers as best as you can, realizing you would have read the book differently if you'd had any idea you'd be taking a test on it.

You look up to see the rest of the book club attendees waiting expectantly for you to finish your quiz, so you mark a few more answers and then wait for whatever happens next.

The hostess pulls out a notebook. "Okay," she says, "let's start brainstorming what we can all write our five-paragraph essays on. Who wants to take a stab at the book's theme?"

By the time you leave book club, you've been assigned to write an essay on the role of duty as it relates to Werner's character. You've also been given a list of hands-on activities to choose from—you could make a diorama, write a diary entry from the perspective of Etienne, or draw a map of Marie Laure's steps through the city of Paris.

On your way home that night, you realize that the book club is really just a way to demonstrate that you've read the book. There's no meaningful discussion happening there, no relationships being formed with other attendees, no deep dive into the murky and beautiful waters of a well-written story. You are assigned tasks only to prove that you did, indeed, read the book.

Check this book off the list—you've "done" it. Now on to a new one.

Would you go back to such a book club? Would you be itching to reread the novel in your free time, call your best friend and ask if she has gotten to the part you're dying to talk about, the part that turned you inside out? Would you—after completing the quiz, writing the essay, building the diorama—feel that the book was one of your life companions? Would you say the book changed you? Formed you? Challenged you?

Or would you simply feel like you had "done the book"?

This is exactly how we treat our children's reading lives, and yet we wonder why they view reading as something to be done for school, for a grade, for a checklist.

All of these—from the comprehension quiz (testing to see if you actually read the story and understood it) to the five-paragraph essay (dissecting the book's theme) to "creative" projects like making a diorama or creating a map—are typical assignments that tend to accompany the books our kids read.

We literally school the love of reading right out of our kids, and then we worry because they aren't taken up with a voracious love of literature and a burning desire to enjoy reading for pleasure.

What would happen, I wonder, if we started treating our kids' reading lives the way we treat our own? What if we were to get out of the way and let the book work its magic on the child without interfering, without telling him how to think about it, without insisting that he parrot back facts or agree with us on the theme? What if, rather than obsessing over whether a child "did" the book, we let our kids meet great ideas, make connections, think for themselves, and experience what it means to be fully human, fully alive, through the great ideas and great characters they encounter in stories?

• • • • •

We literally school the love of reading right out of our kids, and then we worry because they aren't taken up with a voracious love of literature and a burning desire to enjoy reading for pleasure.

Don't misunderstand me here. I'm not suggesting that a teacher or parent never assign schoolwork related to a book. I *am* suggesting, however, that delight must play an important role. If we want to raise kids who will be lifelong readers, then we would do well to take a page from *real* adult readers—those who read for the sheer joy and thrill of it.

The adults I know who read for pleasure do not make dioramas, take comprehension quizzes, or write five-paragraph essays on a story's main conflict or theme. Real readers enjoy books that pique their interest and curiosity. They talk about them with friends. Sometimes they join book clubs. At those book club meetings, they might enjoy food and drink while discussing open-ended questions. They ask questions that help everyone think more deeply about the book and about what the author might have been trying to say. Questions about what the book might be saying to *us*.

Real readers get lost in stories. Sometimes they are burning to talk about them with others; sometimes they just read and ponder the questions by themselves. They may dog-ear the pages, jot down passages from the book in their journals, or underline and scribble in the margins. Real readers engage with books in a way that fuels curiosity, inspires connection, and provides enjoyment.

I read Chaim Potok's *The Chosen* when I was in school, but I don't remember much of it. I remember slogging through the book, trying to find snippets of text I could use to build the argument in my persuasive essay. I remember trying to note random details that I thought might show up on the Friday quiz. I don't remember much else. I have no desire to reread it as an adult, though many people I love and trust call it one of the best books they've ever read.

Are the books *you* wrote reports on as a child the same books for which you have a resounding fondness decades later? Are they the books you can't wait to read with your children, the books you associate with your happiest childhood memories?

Surely a child who loves stories, whose life has been richly bathed in them, who has had many conversations about the characters and quests in the stories she's read, will have no trouble taking apart a piece of literature to analyze it in college. But dissecting the book won't be her natural inclination. And we don't want it to be! There is a time and a place for literary analysis—for charting plots and noting character arcs. But I am not at all convinced that home is that place. Home is where we fall in love with books. Home is the *only* place in which our children have a fighting chance of falling in love with books.

• • • •

Home is the *only* place in which our children have a fighting chance of falling in love with books.

We already know what happens to kids whose parents don't see pleasure and enjoyment as the main reason to read, whose parents think the primary purpose of reading is for academic success. Those kids simply don't read.

EXTREME MEASURES

Jonathan Auxier's mother was concerned about her son's lack of interest in reading for fun, so when he was a young boy, she pulled him out of school, intent on turning him into a reader.

"I came from a family of serious readers," Jonathan said.[8] "I myself knew *how* to read, but I didn't enjoy it very much—I guess there were just other things that I enjoyed more. It was not an activity that brought me joy."

His mother panicked. For any of her children not to read for pure enjoyment and delight simply wasn't an option in their home. She decided to start homeschooling Jonathan during his third-grade year, and the main requirement was that he read for three hours per day.

Now, Jonathan wasn't told that his mother had pulled him out of school in order to help him fall in love with books. But she wisely realized that Jonathan would only learn to love reading if he disassociated reading with schoolwork. He needed plenty of time for reading, and he needed the opportunity to choose books *he* wanted to read—not just books that were assigned to him. She also knew that Jonathan needed to take on the identity of a reader for himself. She couldn't do that for him. All she could do was set up the circumstances to make it more likely to happen.

And happen it did.

"When I came back to traditional school, I was a year older, to be fair—but I was also a very strong reader," Jonathan said. "My mother's move to pull me out of school was certainly the intervention that turned me into a reader."

Jonathan Auxier is now an award-winning writer of middle-grade novels—you'll find *Peter Nimble and His Fantastic Eyes* in one of the booklists in part three of this book. Clearly, his mother gave him more than just an opportunity to become a reader. She gave him an opportunity to form a deep and lasting love for both words and stories.

You probably don't have complete control over all of your kids' interactions with books, especially as they relate to schoolwork. Your child's teacher likely assigns book reports, comprehension quizzes, and other book-related assignments. No matter where your child does his academic learning, though, one thing is true: you *can* shape the atmosphere in your home. You decide the way books are chosen, discussed, and engaged with at home. And that atmosphere means a whole lot. Home, remember, is where our kids fall in love with books.

A parent's attitude about books makes a huge difference in the reading life of a child, regardless of where that child goes to school or what kind of literary education he or she receives. So what's a parent to do? How do we create an environment where we communicate enjoyment of books, curiosity about the ideas they contain, and a desire to connect with our kids? We create a book club culture in the home.

HOW TO CREATE A BOOK CLUB CULTURE AT HOME

Let's try that book club scenario again. This time, you arrive at your friend's house to be greeted by a warm embrace and flickering candlelight. You drop into the plush sofa and catch up for a few minutes with the other friends who are gathered there. The host sets a bowl of tortilla chips and mango salsa on the table and pours chilled Riesling into glasses.

Casually, she shifts the conversation over to the book, leading the discussion by asking an open-ended question. You aren't being quizzed on how much you know or don't know—you're thinking about the book in ways you didn't think of on your own. You're making connections you hadn't made on your own, listening to insights that never occurred to you. You offer your own perspective on which character was the most cowardly, or which character grew the most, or how this book reminded you of the book you read last summer. You toss around ideas about what the characters really want and what they are afraid of.

You leave the book club feeling like you experienced the book a little more fully by being here. You experienced your friendships a little more fully, too, because you were able to get a peek into the minds and souls of your friends as they discussed the parts that made them weep or laugh, caught them off-guard, pleased or scared them. The way one of your friends described the scene where Marie Laure is hiding at the top of the house makes you want to go back home and reread the book because you didn't see all the things she saw. You didn't make the connections she made. You want to see if the book whispers something new to you this time around.

You leave book club feeling richer.

That is what a book club is for—to connect us more deeply with what we read, to help us bond more meaningfully with the people in our lives, to leave us feeling as though we've only shaken hands with the story. We're now hungry to go back and spend more time with this book—or another one.

A really good story can't be properly experienced or examined under the scrutiny of a magnifying glass. It can't be tested, quizzed, or five-paragraph-essayed into our soul. A good story gives shape to the human experience and touches us in our innermost places. It picks us up right where we are and leaves us somewhere else—changed, transformed, more awake and alive and aware. We leave better off than we came. Richer.

Katherine Paterson has written many award-winning children's books about big and deep issues. Tragedy, comedy, death, loneliness, hope, fear, sorrow—all have a place in her rich and imaginative books. But Paterson doesn't want her books to be used in a classroom to teach vocabulary or test comprehension levels.

"When I write a story, it is not an attempt to make children good or wise—nobody but God can do that, and even God doesn't do it without the child's cooperation," she says. "I am trying in a book simply to give children a place where they may find rest for their weary souls."[9]

• • • • •

A good story gives shape to the human experience and touches us in our innermost places. It picks us up right where we are and leaves us somewhere else—changed, transformed, more awake and alive and aware.

If we compare the average kid's classroom experience with our own book club meetings, we'll get a sense for how to treat our children's reading lives more like our own. We'll create a book club culture at home in an organic, simple, natural way. This is not to suggest that you must replace your child's literary experience in the classroom in order to live out a richer one at home (although admittedly, that's what I've chosen to do with my own kids). But your home can be infused with a book club spirit. Your own attitude about books and reading can shift to allow every member of the family more time and space for reading at whim, more reading for the sheer pleasure of it.

FOOD, GLORIOUS FOOD

Try something for me. Bake a pan of brownies. As the scent drives everyone in your home toward the kitchen in hopeful curiosity, place some small plates and napkins on the table, and pour a pitcher of milk. Set those brownies—luscious, gooey, piping hot—in the center of the table, and open a book. It can be anything: a picture book, middle-grade fiction, a poem. It doesn't really matter *which* book it is; just start reading it aloud.

I can nearly guarantee you will have a table full of people listening in, and they will remember—even well into the future—that you read it with brownies. They will very likely look back on that book with fondness.

I have never been to a grown-up book club meeting that didn't include food, and yet I so often make my kids' book-reading sessions feel more like a classroom than a book club.

Why no treats? Why no snacks? Why not throw a big picnic blanket on the grass in the backyard and let everyone dig into a ginormous bowl of popcorn and sip Capri Suns? Why not set the table with china and pass around tea and scones? Why not pull out a package of store-bought cookies and paper plates and gather everyone at the table for a few moments of rest and reading?

I don't always give my kids snacks while I'm reading aloud, but I do try to manage it on occasion, especially if I'm having trouble wooing anyone into read-aloud time, or if our relationships and interactions have been particularly fraught. Food is comfort, and comfort is a wonderful thing to associate with read-aloud time.

My husband speaks fondly of his own family's game nights when he was growing up. They played Monopoly, Risk, and other classic board games. But when he tells me stories of his family's game nights, the games themselves play a minor role in his memory. He mostly remembers the tea, the little bowl of sugar, the gravy boat filled with milk, and the soft, light, sweet coffee cake his mother served.

Tea and coffee cake became a symbol for game night. When

my husband drinks tea from a fancy cup, stirs in a swirl of milk, and drops in a pinch of sugar, he thinks of game night. He remembers family time, warm and comforting.

We can do the same with stories. You don't need to make coffee cake every time you read aloud, of course, but it wouldn't hurt. Popcorn is my own go-to. It's quick and easy and everyone likes it, so I often make a giant bowl and put it in the middle of the table while I read.

It can be simple—a box of crackers, store-bought cookies, sliced fruit, a bowl of grapes. Sharing food and gathering around the table means community, friendship, love, laughter, and warmth. That's what we're going for, right?

Do we have the courage to admit that the main purpose of reading *may* in fact be for joy, for the sake of itself? Affection is of great importance when it comes to making connections with our kids through books. When we demonstrate interest in the things that our kids are interested in—and that includes the stories they like—we are communicating love to them.

What I wish I could say to that mom at the library, the one who told her ten-year-old daughter to put *The Penderwicks* aside in favor of something that would "count" for school, is this: Go get a copy yourself. Read it with her, just for fun. Not because it "counts," not because she gets credit for it in class, and not even because it will make her a better human being for having read it (though it might).

Read it to waste time with her. Read it for the single purpose of getting lost in a good story alongside your child. Read it to connect. The memories she'll store from the time you spent that didn't count for anything other than the joy of connecting—those are the memories she'll carry with her long into the future. Read with your daughter at whim.

When we create a book club culture at home, we send a crucial message to our children. We communicate that their reading life matters and that it ought to be a source of joy and delight to them. We allow them the freedom and ability to engage with ideas in the place we want them to love most of all: home. Perhaps best of all, we give them a fighting chance of falling madly in love with the reading life.

Chapter 7

DEBUNK FIVE MYTHS

• • • •

Sometimes it is necessary to paint the sky black in order to show how beautiful is the prick of light . . . When a child reads the last sentence of my stories, I hope he or she drifts to sleep with a glow in their hearts and a warmth in their bones, believing that all shall be well, and all shall be well, and all manner of things shall be well.

Andrew Peterson[1]

The small, sparkling lake was a hidden pocket of cool, dark water tucked into the hillside of towering pines. I sat in my beach chair, sipping iced tea as the kids tiptoed out to the end of a little rock jetty and started catching minnows with small, handheld nets. Each child stood still as a statue, waiting for just the right moment before dipping his or her net into the water—*whoosh!* A fish squiggled into its captor's net for a moment while the children cheered. They compared each minnow's size to its predecessor's, gave it a name, then lowered it back into the lake to set it free.

I hope we do this all day, I thought to myself, flipping open the novel I had optimistically tucked into my beach bag.

"It's . . . not . . . working!" Clara exclaimed in frustration, her four-year-old body stiff, fists clenched. She had been mimicking the older kids' every move nearly perfectly—leaning over the lake, holding herself still, and watching for a sign of movement in the water before lowering the net for a catch. Each time, however, her net came up empty and her cheeks flushed in frustration.

I inched out to the jetty and knelt down to see if I could help. Immediately, I saw the problem. Her net had a hole.

"Good news—we can fix it," I said, taking Clara's hand and leading her back through the sand. We stopped underneath the deck, where life jackets, lake toys, and dozens of multicolored pool noodles were stashed in a giant, disorganized heap.

"You can't catch a fish with a broken net!" I told her, switching out the net she had been using for one without a hole.

Clara grabbed the net from my hand and turned, running straight back to the other children at the jetty, back to her task. This time, she would be victorious.

USING A BROKEN NET

That day at the lake, Clara was motivated by a strong desire to catch a fish. She was inspired by the older kids' technique and was intent on following suit—executing the right posture, actions, and exact speed of net-swooshing, dipping, and lifting. But she couldn't catch a fish because something else was keeping her from success: her net was broken. And when we have a broken tool, motivation can only take us so far.

If reading aloud really *is* the most effective way to use our time and energy as parents, then why don't we do it more often? Why does it seem so difficult to pull off? Even the highly motivated parent (raising my hand here) struggles to make read-aloud time happen as often as they'd like.

I've noticed something curious as I've talked to families about their reading lives. A whole lot of us have the motivation we need. We want what's best for our kids, after all. We want them to see themselves as heroes in their own stories, to succeed academically, to become kind and compassionate. We aren't lacking for motivation.

But we do have a tendency to overcomplicate things. I once heard Dr. Meg Meeker say that many parents come to her pediatric practice worried about their kids' self-esteem. They have all kinds of plans for how to fix it, she said—signing up for martial arts, the swim team, or art classes.[2] Carting their children around to more activities seems like the best answer, because then kids will have the opportunity to get good at something, to excel. But Dr. Meeker doesn't think this is the best way to boost a child's self-esteem.

A child will likely have great self-esteem if she believes her parents like her and want to spend time with her. A better alternative, then, is to spend time enjoying our children and communicating that enjoyment clearly, according to Dr. Meeker.[3] It turns out it's a lot cheaper than schlepping them to classes and clubs all over town. It's a whole lot easier, too. I don't know about you, but whipping out a set of Uno cards and spending an hour around a card table drinking hot chocolate with my pre-teen is a lot more appealing than grabbing dinner on the run so I can haul him downtown to rock-climbing lessons on a dark Tuesday night.

This tendency to overcomplicate problems we encounter in parenting is a common reaction for many of us. It's no different when it comes to reading aloud.

What keeps us from making meaningful and lasting connections with our kids is not a lack of motivation or drive, but rather our unfortunate tendency to overcomplicate things. This happens most often because we believe five myths about sharing books with our kids. Those myths hold us back from making progress in the one area that will have a more significant impact on our kids than any other. In short, we're believing lies that are making our already difficult job of parenting harder than necessary.

Until we can get clear about what's true in our family's read-aloud life, this whole shindig is going to be a lot more difficult than it needs to be.

> • • • • •
> A child will likely have great self-esteem if she believes her parents like her and want to spend time with her.

MYTH #1: IF YOU WANT READING ALOUD TO MAKE A DIFFERENCE, YOU NEED TO DO A LOT OF IT

Fact: If you find yourself waiting until you have thirty free minutes to read with your kids, there is a good chance you won't read to them very often (or maybe at all). So many distractions are vying for our attention each day, keeping us from our most important work. On an average day, I'm running multiple loads of laundry, preparing meals for a family of eight, teaching my son math, editing my high schooler's essay, tidying the house four million times, chasing down three small children, answering five phone calls, getting behind on email, tending to a long to-do list for work, trying to connect with my husband, and running one kid to the orthodontist while I make a snappy trip to the grocery store for milk and bread. Again.

Some simple math can be helpful here. Let's say I read ten minutes per day with my kids. Just ten minutes. I can find ten minutes in most any day—even my busiest days. I might have to skip sweeping the kitchen, folding a pile of laundry, or one of my Facebook scrolling sessions, but I'm quite certain I can scare up ten minutes somewhere in my day. If I read for ten minutes every day, I'll have read with my kids for sixty hours over the course of a year. Sixty hours!

Whenever someone tells me to do something "every day," however, I find myself breaking out in a fresh set of hives. *Floss every day. Exercise every day. Pray every day. Eat something green every day.*

Every day. Those two words alone fill me with anxiety. How can I add *anything* to my docket every day? And now I need to carve out time to read aloud every day, too?

Actually, no. And for the record, I'll say it as clearly as I can: *You do not need to read aloud to your children every day.*

If I read for ten minutes every *other* day with my kids, that's only about thirty-five minutes per week. Doable, right? I'm breathing a little easier now. I can imagine myself getting to read-aloud time every other day or so, even if we're on vacation, I'm sick for a few days, we're extra busy during basketball playoffs, or I'm overloaded at work.

• • • •

You do not need to read aloud to your children every day.

Here's where this gets good: ten minutes every other day for an entire year equals thirty hours of reading aloud over the course of a year. That's a tremendous amount of reading. You could read aloud the entire Chronicles of Narnia or over two hundred picture books in thirty hours. You could read every single Ramona Quimby book by Beverly Cleary *plus* three or four books by Roald Dahl.

Don't have thirty minutes to read with your kids? You don't need it. Try ten. You can arrive ten minutes early to soccer practice and read aloud in the car while you wait, or stay at the dinner table ten minutes longer so you can read a bit of *Charlie and the Chocolate Factory* or *Heidi*. Put the kids to bed a few minutes later, or wake them up for school a few minutes earlier.

Next time you catch yourself thinking that you don't have enough time to read aloud with your kids, stop and tell yourself the truth. You can find ten minutes, and that's all it takes. If you want reading aloud to make a difference, you don't need to do a ton of it. You just need to do a little bit of it over a long stretch of time. It all adds up.

MYTH #2: IT ONLY COUNTS AS READING ALOUD IF YOU DO THE READING YOURSELF

My friend Laura sent me a last-minute text: *We're about to head out on the road. I'm kind of dreading it.*

She and her husband were packing up their three kids for a road trip to Chattanooga, Tennessee, and she was worried that her kids would either be glued to devices or bickering the whole way. I texted back a quick reply, recommending that she download some audiobooks. My phone pinged again: *Suggestions?*

I sent a short list of options that would engage all three of her kids, hopefully without driving her husband up the wall, then said if they hadn't heard *Poppy* by Avi yet, it would be my first choice.

That was all I heard from Laura until they arrived back home a week later. "Our entire family was on the edge of their seats the whole time," Laura said. The seven-year-old hardly fussed, and one of the big kids cried, "No, Mom! You can't stop there!" when they stopped for lunch and a bathroom break.

"It was crazy. It was awesome. The kids didn't even *ask* for their devices," Laura said, laughing.

Somewhere along the line, we've convinced ourselves that audiobooks don't count as real reading. The magic of a read-aloud is achieved when we share stories together. It's the shared experience itself that makes the biggest impact, whether the voice doing the actual reading is your own, your spouse's, or a professional actor's via an audiobook. Children still benefit from correct and sophisticated language patterns coming in through the ear, and they're inspired to become heroes of their own stories.

It gets better, too. Your kids will gain the benefits of reading aloud a whole lot more often when you are free of having to do all the reading yourself. Think of how many more books you'll be able to share with your kids this way! You can play audiobooks in the car, during a meal, or while the whole family pitches in to fold a big pile of laundry (my own favorite way to tackle that arduous chore).

Audiobooks count. Sure, there's something nostalgic and heartwarming about a child's ears and memories being filled with their mother's or father's voice. Jennifer Trafton, author of *The Rise and Fall of Mount Majestic* and *Henry and the Chalk Dragon*, told me once that Aslan's voice will always sound like her dad. He spent hours reading the Chronicles of Narnia aloud to her when she was young. That's beautiful, isn't it? If you can do the reading aloud yourself, then by all means do! But if you *also* include audiobooks, you'll fit in more reading aloud than you could otherwise.

There is so much to be gained by a family enjoying audiobooks together or by a child who can listen to audiobooks on his or her own. My own son, a late reader, listened to dozens of audiobooks in his seventh and eighth years during our afternoon Quiet Reading Hour. While his older sisters read alone, he played audiobooks from the *Redwall* series in his room on an old CD player while also building LEGO creations. Just imagine how many more books he was able to "read" that way.

An added benefit of using audiobooks is that they allow a skilled narrator to draw us into the story. Remember Rebecca Bellingham reading *Charlotte's Web* to her class back in chapter 4? Her students were able to get lost in the book because she did the hard work of decoding the words on the page and reading with the right rhythm and pace. The same thing happens for us with audiobooks. Mark Twain's stories, for example, can be difficult to read aloud if you're unfamiliar with the pronunciation of the dialect. Likewise, the work of Charles Dickens is positively exquisite when read by a British narrator. We allow ourselves the privilege of getting lost in the story when we listen to a well-read audiobook.

MYTH #3: LIGHT BOOKS DON'T COUNT

I remember the book that turned me into a real reader. I had been reading on my own for a while by the time I stumbled across Roald Dahl's *Matilda*. Nevertheless, when I finished reading it, I was a different human being than when I had begun. I wanted more. I was hungry. I suddenly had an insatiable thirst for books and for the ideas and stories inside them. This is a pivotal moment for each of us, and it usually happens when we read something light, delightful, and completely enjoyable—not when we're slogging through text that's difficult to read or hard to understand.

Most of the people I know who fell in love with books as children didn't fall in love while reading *The Hound of the Baskervilles* or unabridged versions of *The Adventures of Tom Sawyer* or *The Swiss Family Robinson*. Love for those came later (if at all), but that initial love—that moment of transformation when we progress from being a child who doesn't read much to one who reads voraciously—usually happens with lighter fare. I've asked countless *Read-Aloud Revival* listeners to tell me which books turned them into readers, and this is what they tell me: Cam Jansen, The Hardy Boys, Nancy Drew, The Babysitter's Club . . . Their eyes twinkle as they recall nights spent with a flashlight under the covers, flipping through collections of Garfield, Calvin & Hobbes, or Marvel and DC comic books. They tell me they read every single Trixie Belden book they could find, every copy of Nate the Great they could get their hands on.

Of course, saying that light reading matters and that it has a place doesn't devalue more difficult reading. Classics—those old, wonderful books that have stood the test of time—are among the greatest literature ever written. Far be it from me to minimize the impact such books have on us as individuals and as a culture.

What we feed our bodies matters, and what we feed our souls matters, too. This is true for us, but even more so for our kids, who are discovering who they are—and Whose they are—as they grow.

Sometimes, however, we find ourselves valuing classics and rich literature to the point of excluding other, lighter fare. If we cringe when our kids devour series books or gravitate toward the lighter, fluffier books that are so prolific in our local libraries and bookshops, we're missing something important. Lighter books have their own special part to play in the growth and development of young readers.

When Audrey was twelve, she couldn't get enough of the Cupcake Diaries by Coco Simon. Her reading level far exceeded those books, and it occurred to me that perhaps she should be reading more edifying, nourishing fare. I considered telling her to lay off the series and choose something meatier. I'm so glad I didn't. Cupcake Diaries did for her what The Babysitter's Club did for me in my own tween years. She read them voraciously, gaining fluency and speed while discovering that reading is enjoyable for its own sake. Her binge on Cupcake Diaries books turned out to be short-lived and didn't impede her literary taste as an older teen whatsoever. These days she's likely to pick up Louisa May Alcott or Jane Austen of her own accord.

Likewise, my daughter Allison gobbled up Rainbow Magic books as soon as she could tackle them on her own. They were like candy, and she couldn't get enough of them. I'm convinced those books turned her into a reader. By reading a copious amount of easy books, she became better at the *skill* of reading—a skill that will serve her well all through her life. Now, though she is only a young teen, I often catch her reading books far beyond a typical teenager's reading level. She chooses literary classics for the sheer fun of it. Reading piles of easy books during those earlier years didn't hurt her. In fact, it helped her identify as a *real reader.* And that can make all the difference in a child's reading life.

Most of us would do well to realize that any time we spend reading with our kids is time well spent, regardless of whether the books are on particular booklists or meet a certain literary standard. Sometimes we forget this very important truth: the kids matter more than the books. The books themselves are important, but only insofar as they nurture the image bearer before us.

We'll get into how to choose excellent books in chapter 9. For now, it's helpful to be aware that you don't have to limit your kids to certain books. Light books count. Hard books count. Current bestsellers count. Classics count. They all have their place in the tapestry of a child's reading life.

• • • • • •

Light books count. Hard books count. Current bestsellers count. Classics count. They all have their place in the tapestry of a child's reading life.

MYTH #4: MY KIDS SHOULD BE SITTING STILL WHILE I READ ALOUD TO THEM

Anyone with a wiggly child knows that expecting him to sit still while you read aloud is something of a lost cause. It boggles my mind that my son—the one who is now engaging a set of army guys in battle, now standing on his head in the corner, now drawing a picture, now wrestling a little brother, now getting a drink of water—will remember what we've read aloud better than just about anyone else in the room.

Studies show that for many children, actively engaging in something with their hands helps them listen better. For many kids, the propensity to move while engaging in focused brain-work is best facilitated, not quashed. Give them something to do with their hands, and their brains are suddenly free to focus and learn.

I asked Dr. Michael Gurian, a renowned family counselor, founder of the Gurian Institute, and *New York Times* bestselling author of twenty-eight books on various aspects of childhood development, about this very thing. He said that for some kids, information can go deeper into their brains when the child physically moves around. Those kids listen *better* when they get up and move because of how their brains are wired. So it's not a problem when they start to fidget—in fact, for many kids, it's actually better! Their desire to move indicates more advanced processing of what they hear while we read. Statistically, Dr. Gurian says this is more often true for boys than for girls. You can learn more about this in his book, *Boys and Girls Learn Differently*.

My own six children are almost always doing something with their hands while they listen to read-alouds. Messing with Play-Doh, coloring with crayons or markers, practicing calligraphy, sculpting with clay, building with LEGOs, trying their hand at crochet—everybody usually has something going on.

You may be amazed at how much better your kids listen, how much longer they stay focused during read-aloud time, and how much more peaceful the experience is for *you*, the reader, when you free up your kids to move around during reading time.

My kids colored stained-glass coloring books from Dover Publications, for example, while I read Gloria Whelan's beautiful book, *Listening for Lions*. They finger-knitted long strings of colored yarn when I read about the Sager children's epic journey on the Oregon Trail in Honore Morrow's *On to Oregon!*. They used window markers to fill up our dining room windows with drawings as I read Sid Fleischman's *By the Great Horn Spoon!* (one of our favorite read-alouds ever—definitely add that one to your list for kids seven and up).

You'll find lists of activities your child can do while you read aloud, depending on their age, in the final four chapters of this book.

Your kids don't need to sit still to get the most out of your read-aloud time. In fact, they may get *more* out of it if you let them fidget or doodle while you read.

MYTH #5: IF IT DOESN'T LOOK THE WAY I IMAGINED IT WOULD, I MUST BE DOING SOMETHING WRONG

When I first sought to make reading aloud a regular pillar of our family life, I had visions of sitting on the hearth, reading *Robinson Crusoe* while my children sat on the floor around my feet doing productive, inspiring, creative things. Whittling, maybe. Or knitting a blanket.

But reading aloud doesn't look like that in my home. On our best days, I've got the kids around the dining room table, actively engaged with their hands while I read. Often, the watercolor paint cups spill. Somebody kicks someone else's leg under the table. The three-year-old decides to shout the word *poop* every three minutes. (What? That doesn't happen at your house?) Solicitors knock on the door, heedless of my NO SOLICITING sign. By the time I send the unwelcome visitors away and return to my seat, I've lost half of my audience.

The families I know who read aloud most consistently (and therefore who get the most benefits) tell me that reading aloud doesn't look perfect in their homes either; it rarely (if ever) looks like they originally imagined it would.

Kids fight over couch cushions. Someone complains that the preschooler is making too much noise. The toddler runs off and starts shoving Hot Wheels down the toilet before you even notice he's gone. A kid jumps up every couple of minutes to sharpen one of his colored pencils, or another one wanders away right at the most climactic scene in the book. There are endless interruptions and constant rounds of bickering.

When read-aloud time doesn't look like we originally hoped, we begin to doubt that it's giving us any of those wonderful benefits we discussed in part 1.

But here's the thing: it still works. Even when it's noisy, messy, and more chaotic than you'd like it to be, it works. Even when kids are grumbling, complaining, and don't seem to be listening, it works. When we read aloud to our kids in spite of the fact that it looks much different from our initial vision, we're stepping out in faith. If I can tell you one thing in this entire chapter, it is this: keep stepping out.

When idealistic visions pop into your head, when you find

yourself thinking about that Instagram post by the mom whose kids all appear perfectly content to listen to her read a classic for hours, stop yourself. Shut down the idealistic visions, because when you're reading aloud, even when it looks imperfect, *you* are going all-in. And you'll never regret it. You won't say, twenty years from now, "Dang, if I could do the parenting thing over again, I'd read less to my kids."

It's worth it even when it looks nothing like a gorgeous magazine photo op. It's worth it, perhaps, *because* it looks nothing like a gorgeous magazine photo op. It looks like living and loving and going all-in. After all, that's exactly what it is.

• • • • •

You won't say, twenty years from now, "Dang, if I could do the parenting thing over again, I'd read less to my kids."

I'm much like four-year-old Clara, trying to catch fish with a broken net. I'm motivated. I'm using good booklists, piling my kids onto the couch, *trying* to make meaningful and lasting connections with them. But buying into any of these myths is like trying to fish with a broken net. It doesn't work. I do the work but feel frustrated that it doesn't look or feel like I thought it would.

Clara just needed a new net. I, however, need to swap out my belief that I have to do tons of reading aloud for the belief that a little bit every other day will make an impact. I need to embrace audiobooks and the wonderful boost they can give my family's reading life. I need to give my family freedom to read light books, freedom to move and wiggle and fidget when I read, and above all, I need to realize that even if it doesn't look anything like I thought it would, it's still good. Still worth it. Still making an impact in ways I can hardly imagine.

SET YOURSELF UP FOR SUCCESS

• • • •

To be at home with books, children need book-loving homes.

Elizabeth Wilson, *Books Children Love*

It was an unusually warm spring day, and I had no intention of letting it get away from us. I grabbed Jennifer Trafton's middle-grade novel, *The Rise and Fall of Mount Majestic*, nabbed a box of popsicles from the freezer, and told all the kids to meet me on a picnic blanket in the backyard in approximately three minutes.

The little ones made a beeline for the door, ready to cash in on an unexpected afternoon treat. I settled myself on the blanket, unwrapped popsicles, then called inside to the big kids once again, "Come on, guys! Read-aloud time!"

"Coming!"

"Be there in a minute!"

"On my way!"

Clara dropped her popsicle in the grass and erupted in a meltdown. I snatched it up and ran inside to clean it off under the faucet, watching bits of grass and debris float down the drain.

"Kids! Read-aloud blanket! Backyard! Now!" I called.

I heard a ruffling of papers coming from the office, the whir of the electric pencil sharpener.

"We're coming, Mom! Just getting a few things to do!"

I huffed back out to the yard, noticing that the other kids' popsicles were already nearly gone. They had slurped them halfway, sticky syrup sliding down their arms. Emerson held his drippy treat tauntingly over his twin brother's head, watching as the bright red juice made its way slowly into his brother's left ear. A squall erupted from Becket, as he felt the goo make its way down.

The three big kids plunked down on the picnic blanket at last, but not before the twins complained about their sticky fingers.

"Go grab baby wipes, please," I told the oldest. The phone in my back pocket vibrated with a text from my husband: *Can you please send the new bank account password? Trying to take care of some bills.* Then the doorbell rang, and all three littles hopped up to see who it was.

I laughed at the absurdity of it all, if only to keep myself from crying. Wasn't this supposed to be easy? Wasn't this supposed to be *enjoyable*? How on earth was this read-aloud thing going to help me create lasting, lifelong bonds with my kids?

In the last chapter, we dismantled the myth that read-aloud time should look like it does in our imaginations. The reality is that it just doesn't, at least not most of the time. But it *can* be more peaceful—or at least less chaotic than the experience I just described—if we set ourselves up for success.

Here's what I know: a read-aloud lifestyle isn't going to happen in our homes by accident. You and me—parents in a busy, fast-paced world crammed full of distractions—have to be intentional about making reading aloud a regular part of family life.

We need a few strategies to help us make read-aloud time happen more often than it doesn't, as well as strategies to help us enjoy it. We know it's important—wildly so!—but we don't want it to become one more item on our to-do list, one more dreaded task crammed into an already-crowded schedule. We also need strategies to deal with screens, because all of us are facing a tremendous competitor for our time and attention—and so are our kids. We need to set ourselves up for success.

• • • • •

You and me—parents in a busy, fast-paced world crammed full of distractions—have to be intentional about making reading aloud a regular part of family life.

LESSONS THROUGH A LENS

It was a gift for my thirtieth birthday, and I was terrified of it. Sure, I enjoyed taking pictures—and who wouldn't want to learn how to take amazing ones when there's about to be another newborn in the house? But a DSLR camera is an expensive birthday gift, so I welcomed it with a combination of both awe and terror. *How will I ever learn to use it? What if my talent and skill never measure up to the worthiness of this piece of equipment?* Surely my husband would regret making such a large purchase. Surely I could learn photography on something far less expensive than this beautiful piece of machinery.

I thanked Andy for the gift, then filled my library holds queue with every book I could find on photography. I read up on how to take still shots, motion shots, baby shots. I learned about aperture and bokeh and ISOs. I followed a trillion photography blogs and even took an online course. Over the next year, I learned how to use that camera—not like a professional, but perhaps like a skilled amateur. I learned not to be afraid of it. I found my groove, and it ended up being the best birthday gift I've ever received.

Over that year, I realized that even if I read up on photography techniques, it wasn't until I put the book down, picked up the camera, and went out into the front yard to *use* it on the going-to-seed dandelions sprouting in the yard that I really understood it. It wasn't until I started clicking the shutter with regularity that I saw real improvement in my photos.

Experience, it turns out, is the best teacher. The more often I picked up my camera, the better I got. All of those obscure things I was reading about in books, like "open shade" and "hair light," started to make sense. But they only made sense once they had legs on them. I had to start *doing* in order to really get the benefits. YouTube videos, online tutorials, and stacks of books would only take me so far.

I kept my camera close at hand that year. It wasn't natural for me to take pictures constantly. It wasn't my gut reaction when the light filtered into the kitchen just so or a golden hue fell over the backyard.

Instead, I had to set myself up for success. I had to make it easy to grab my camera and start clicking before I saw any real improvement in my photography.

MAKE IT EASY

Most of us want to make meaningful and lasting connections with our kids. If you've read this far, I'm willing to bet that you do, too. I'm also willing to bet you know that the best way to make those connections is by opening up the pages of a book with your child.

Sounds simple, right? And what a relief to know that as

overwhelming and intimidating as this parenting gig is, the most effective way to rock it is to simply sit down with our kids and read from the pages of a book.

But here's what I know: if we don't make it easy to do—if we don't set ourselves up for success—it won't happen. If I don't put the camera on the kitchen counter and keep the battery charged, I'm probably not going to take as many pictures as I'd like to, and if I don't take a few strategic steps to making read-aloud time easy to pull off, I'm probably not going to read with my kids nearly as much as I hope I will, either.

If it's not our default to pick up a book and start reading aloud with our kids, then we can be intentional about making it a habit—about setting ourselves up for success. We can make it easy to read aloud more often.

Keep it handy

When I discovered that taking more pictures was the key to getting better at photography, I knew I needed to make it more habitual for me to pick up my camera. I didn't set a goal for how many times a day I would shoot photos, or how many snapshots I wanted to capture each week. The method I chose was far simpler—leave my camera out where I would see it often, and grab it whenever I could.

Every day, I walk by my kitchen counter an untold number of times. It's why my husband's stack of *things* that are piled up in a corner of the kitchen (which I lovingly and passive-aggressively call the Dump Station) drives me crazy. I look at it all day. The kitchen counter is probably the busiest, most frequented place in our entire house. It's where I stand to prepare food, gather my thoughts, transition to the next task, open the mail, correct schoolwork, sign permission forms. It's my command center.

If I strategically leave my read-aloud book on the counter, there's a good chance I will see it a bazillion times throughout the day. There's also a good chance that at one point or another, I'll end up deciding to read aloud.

You know how, when you're trying to eat healthier, it's helpful to chop vegetables and keep them ready in the fridge? If the first thing I see when I open my fridge is a pile of celery sticks, I'm more likely to choose them when I'm hankering for a snack.

Our read-aloud books are hardly celery sticks (ahem), but the same idea applies: keep your read-aloud handy so it's easy to grab. You want to see it often. That way you get a constant reminder that this is something you want to get to *today*.

Plunk a few read-aloud books on your kitchen counter in the morning, and see if that doesn't inspire you to read a little more often than if the books were tucked away, alphabetized on the bookshelves, or stored neatly in a basket under the table in the living room. Put your books front and center. Keep them handy. Then you don't have to go out of your way when it's time to read aloud, because the books are right there.

Peg it to your day

Habits are such because they happen without our thinking them through. There is no decision-making with a habit. Every night when I'm getting ready for bed, I flick on my bedside lamp and turn off the ceiling light. I don't have to think about it—I just do it when I enter my room on my way into the bathroom to wash my face and brush my teeth. When I go downstairs in the morning, I don't stand there deciding whether to have coffee that day (imagine!). I just start the coffeepot. It's a habit.

If you're convinced that reading aloud with your kids is worthy of your time, then the simplest way to make it happen *more* often is by turning it into a habit. The best way I know how to do that is by pegging it to something else that happens every day.

If you attach reading aloud to something you're already doing every day, the chances you'll get to that reading time suddenly skyrocket.

Melissa Wiley, author of several books including the light-hearted middle-grade novel *The Prairie Thief*, said that when her kids were younger, she wanted to read poetry with them. It was hard to fit into the schedule, though, and she found that many weeks, they wouldn't read so much as a single stanza. Then one day, she realized that her kids regularly showed up for breakfast, so she hatched a plan. They started reading poetry together *while* they ate breakfast, and Melissa found that they got to it far more often. It wasn't a habit in her family until it was pegged to breakfast. Then it became habitual, and they began reading more poetry together than they would have otherwise.

Jamie Martin, author of the fabulous book *Give Your Child the World*, pegged read-alouds to dinnertime. While she finished dinner prep, her husband read to the kids at the dinner table to help them wind down from the day's activities and get in a calmer mood. Then Jamie set out the dinner plates, and everyone ate and chatted about their days. Jamie or her husband (whoever finished eating first) then picked up the book again and read for another ten to fifteen minutes. Dinnertime was already a habit in the Martin home, so adding a read-aloud to it just made sense. It also made read-aloud time happen more often.

Meals are a natural peg because they happen every day, and it's usually easy to convince kids to show up when you include food. As a bonus, everyone's mouths are full, so noise can be kept to a minimum (unless you have toddlers, of course, in which case mealtimes may be the *worst* time of day to read aloud). You can decide what works or doesn't work for your family's season of life, and feel free to change it up as needed.

Consider anything that happens with regularity in your family's schedule. A commute to school? A drive to basketball practice? A giant laundry-folding session in the afternoon? Peg a short reading session to something that already happens regularly in your family's life, and you'll find that it's much easier to fit in read-aloud time, even on your busiest days.

The earlier in the day, the better

One winter, when my oldest three children were nine, seven, and five, I discovered it was much easier to woo them out of their warm beds if they knew we would start our day with a read-aloud. We'd get up and stagger out to the kitchen in our pajamas to fill mugs with coffee, tea, or cocoa before gathering on the living room sofas to tuck ourselves under blankets and ease our way into the day with a story. That winter we read *The Wonderful Wizard of Oz, Caddie Woodlawn,* and *Justin Morgan Had a Horse*. These are some of my favorite memories from that year—cozied up bedheads starting our day with story and warmth.

We've added a few more kids since then, and we don't read aloud before breakfast anymore, but reading early in the day has remained the gold standard for me.

I'm a more relaxed, pleasant parent if I can get to the most important things in my day early on. Even if the rest of the day goes awry, I'm happy that we got to our most important thing. Plus, I tend to enjoy books more (and am willing to read longer) if we get to our read-aloud session before I get tired.

Record your progress

I'm reluctant to offer this strategy. Why? Because when I see a need for a change in my parenting, I tend to overhaul everything and make a grand plan. For example, I'll decide we should be spending more time out-of-doors, so I'll look up nature study plans, make a list of possible locations to visit, and rearrange my entire schedule to make time for a weekly hike. Or I'll decide I'm not reading my Bible as often as I should, so I'll make myself a chart, declare that I am now going to get up before dawn to do it, and create an overzealous Bible reading plan.

It's rare that this method works for the long term, however. I tend to keep up my new resolution for a day or two, then fail. That's why I'm hesitant to offer "mark your progress" as a suggested strategy.

When I feel my kids need to be outside more, the best thing to do is tell them to put on their shoes and take them outside for a walk—right then and there. When I haven't spent much time in the Word, the best thing to do is pull out my Bible and spend ten minutes reading from my favorite gospel (John, for the record) on the spot.

If you're frustrated that you haven't been reading aloud with your kids more often, what you probably need to do is grab the kid closest to you at this very moment, and choose a book from the nearest bookshelf. Then read for ten minutes.

I mean it. Got a kid handy? Try it right now. I'll wait.

See? You're a read-aloud parent. You don't need a chart or a plan. You just need ten minutes and the willingness to let whatever else was on your task list next wait its turn while you spend a few minutes investing in someone who means the world to you.

I know there are a lot of human souls who love and are motivated by checklists. I happen to be one of them. That's why

I'm suggesting this as a strategy against my better judgment. I get an adrenaline rush from drawing an X on a calendar or chart, from marking something complete, from progress made visible.

It is said that Jerry Seinfeld was coaching a young comedian on how to improve his jokes. When the burgeoning humorist asked Seinfeld for his best advice, Seinfeld told him this: write new jokes every day. Mark a big X on your calendar when you write new jokes. He told the comedian to see how many X's in a row he could get, making it a goal not to break the chain.

The checklist-y among us can do the same thing with reading aloud. We can make an X on a calendar for each day that we read aloud to at least one of our kids for ten minutes or more. You can actually download a free printable calendar specifically for this purpose at ReadAloudCalendar.com. I keep that year-at-a-glance calendar on my fridge, and whenever I read for ten minutes or more (with any of my kids), I make an X. Mine isn't an unbroken chain, but it hardly matters. At the end of each year, I see all of those X's looking back at me from the calendar, and I know that they add up—that the time was well spent, that I'm a read-aloud mom even when I'm not getting to it every single day. It reminds me that small things matter, that ten minutes a day add up over time to hours and years—a lifetime spent doing the most important thing.

• • • •

It reminds me that small things matter, that ten minutes a day adds up over time to hours and years—a lifetime spent doing the most important thing.

Make a read-aloud shelf

The fourth myth we busted in the previous chapter was this: kids need to sit still while we read to them. The fact is, they don't. Many children actually listen *better* when they fidget or move while doing focused brainwork. I'll bet you know right off the bat which of your kids will benefit most from keeping their hands busy while you read aloud.

In my home, all my kids tend to do something else while I read aloud. Some need it more than others, but it's a regular practice at our house to fiddle and doodle while listening.

But just having a mental list of things your kids can do while you read aloud isn't enough. Remember my experience with the popsicles and the big kids who were taking f-o-r-e-v-e-r to come to read-aloud time? It helps to keep your read-aloud activities in a convenient, easy-to-grab spot.

It's frustrating to look at the clock, notice I have just about twenty minutes to squeeze in some reading aloud before we need to run off to the orthodontist or start dinner prep, and then spend half of that time waiting for my kids to finally join me. It makes for a short, harried, and frustrating read-aloud experience.

My solution for this is a read-aloud shelf. It can also be a drawer, cupboard, or basket, depending on the amount of space you have. On my read-aloud shelf, I keep a set of stackable trays (the kind used in an office) as well as magazine holders. Each child has a stackable tray in which to keep works-in-progress. If they are in the middle of drawing, watercoloring, or hand lettering, for example, they can keep their work-in-progress on their stackable tray.

Magazine holders are filled with easy-to-grab activities. One magazine holder contains several how-to-draw books, blank paper, and sharpened pencils. When it's read-aloud time, all I have to do is grab the whole magazine holder and call the kids to the table. That gets us into our read-aloud time much quicker and with less fumbling around. Other magazine holders hold water-color paper and pans of paints/paintbrushes, cutting workbooks and preschool scissors, Usborne reusable sticker books, etc. Just take whatever items you're already planning on letting your kids engage with for read-aloud time, and group them purposefully and strategically for quick and easy access.

You may even want to give each child his or her own magazine holder. For example, my oldest daughter fills hers with hand-lettering worksheets, workbooks, and calligraphy pens. My twelve-year-old son prefers to stock his with origami paper and supplies for making paper airplanes. If you do this, you (and your kids) won't waste precious read-aloud time gathering supplies or trying to think up what to do.

Take advantage of a captive audience

Audiobooks, you may remember from chapter 7, count. The car is an excellent time to play audiobooks. We get a lot of reading aloud in during our thirty-five-minute drive to and from homeschool co-op every week, and we find that road trips are far more enjoyable when we listen to an audiobook together. When I hear the *Little House* audiobooks read by Cherry Jones (a favorite in our family), I immediately think of long drives across I-90 in Washington State during the year we moved from one side of the state to the other. The endless Washington wheat fields are married, in my mind, to Pa's fiddle and Laura's harrowing descriptions of *The Long Winter* and the town spelling bee. I'll always think of Laura when I'm crossing I-90. I hope my kids will, too.

In the car, your kids are basically a captive audience. If yours (like mine) tend to squabble on road trips, you'll find audiobooks a welcome reprieve. Either way, you'll get more read-alouds in if you use time you're already spending in the car to enjoy a book together.

Books in every room

Research indicates that kids who live in homes where books are plentiful benefit from the mere presence of books. The fact that books are *there* has a lasting positive effect on our kids—on the way they think about home, how they see themselves, and the role they see books playing in their lives.

How a family chooses to spend money says a lot about who they are and what they value. If you want your family to be a reading family, consider letting books make it into your family budget. You can acquire books inexpensively at library book sales, garage sales, and used bookshops. You don't need to fill your bookshelves right away. Owning just a few really wonderful books is better than collecting stacks and stacks of uninspiring, cheap books no one feels compelled to pick up. You can also make it a habit to buy your child a book for each holiday and birthday, making books a prominent part of the way your family celebrates.

A book allowance can help your children grow their own collection. Each month, my own kids are given a small bit of money to spend on books. They look forward to our trips to local bookshops and keep lists of titles they'd like to acquire. Allison loves the quality of Bloomsbury paperbacks, so when she finds another book in E. D. Baker's Wide-Awake Princess series, she uses her book allowance to buy it (even if she's read it before). Audrey has used her allowance to build a gorgeous Lucy Maud Montgomery collection. She's always on the lookout for beautifully covered classics to add to her pretty shelves. Two of my kids literally count down the days every time Brandon Mull gets ready to release another fantasy novel. They don't even try to borrow those books from the library—they know they're going to want to have them on our home shelves, to read and reread over and over again. These books, purchased with their own money and lining their own bookshelves, become a part of their treasured collections. When they move out as adults, they will take formidable libraries with them—libraries that will help them remember who they are and where they came from, long after they leave home.

We send a clear message to our kids when we spend a portion of our family budget on books and when we give books a priority place in our home. We say that they matter, that they are a part of who we are, and that they are a part of our family culture.

THE SIREN SONG OF SCREENS

I used to take my iPhone to bed with me. I'd tell myself I was using it as an alarm clock, and indeed, I would. I would set it down on my nightstand and slip between the sheets, grab my book, plump my pillows, and read a paragraph or three. And then I would remember. *I was going to check on that thing! I'll just peek at my phone real quick.*

Thirty minutes later, I'd find myself cruising Instagram with no recollection of opening the app. I'd be frustrated that I had wasted so much of my reading time scrolling the internet. The phone was just supposed to be my alarm clock!

I'm a thirty-six-year-old woman, identify myself as a reader, make reading goals, and have a TBR (To Be Read) stack about a mile high. I have a strong desire to read a large amount each day, and *still* I find the siren song of the screen almost impossible to resist. My phone dings, pings, vibrates, or even sits on the nightstand completely silent, and somehow, I still feel pulled to divert my eyes and my focus to it.

If this is my own experience as a grown woman, how much more enticing must screens be for our children? How much temptation must they face whenever they sit down with a book—or with anything, for that matter, that is less splashy, scrolly, or sticky than their screens?

Screens are a part of our modern life, and for the vast majority of us, they're here to stay. I know families who ban devices and screens entirely from their home, and if that's you, the rest of this chapter won't be of much help. But if you, like me, want to help your children learn how to navigate a world of screens in a healthy way, allowing for a moderate use of technology and plentiful time for books, then read on.

Dr. Daniel Willingham compares a book to a watermelon: juicy, sweet, delicious. His children enjoy a slice of watermelon quite a lot, delighting in its sticky, drippy goodness on a hot summer day. But if they are offered a piece of candy, they will choose the candy over the watermelon every time.

Here's where we come in as parents. We can offer our kids candy (the screens) on occasion, but it shouldn't always be an option. Watermelon (a book) itself is a sweet delight that nourishes, and is so much easier to enjoy fully when we aren't tempted by candy. By taking the candy off the table at certain times, we relieve our kids of the burden to choose. The freedom we give our kids to enjoy the watermelon comes when their choice to have candy is taken away.

Setting limits on screens

Instead of setting certain times of day when screens are *not* an option, set times of day when screens *are*. We're just switching the default here. If you set certain periods when screens are *not* an option, you're actually opening up the rest of your day to being peppered with requests to use them. But try flipping that and making screens the exception, rather than the rule.

I know families who allow screens only from two to four in the afternoon, or from seven to eight in the evening, for example. The rest of the time, the rule is, "No screens—don't even ask."

For the parent weary of hearing "Can I watch . . . ?" or "Can I play . . . ?" or the one who is just plain tired of seeing a teenager texting friends or scrolling social media, this is a welcome reprieve.

If, for example, the rule is no screens except from six to eight in the evening, then our kids are freed from their desire to engage with screens before six, if only because they know they can't satisfy the desire and so they might as well do something else.

I find rules like this helpful when I'm trying to curb my own use of screens, as well. Only *you* can decide when and how much time is appropriate for your kids to have a screen option. Just realize that whenever screen time is allowed, you are essentially asking them if they'd prefer a slice of watermelon or a candy bar. Don't expect your child to choose the watermelon when candy is there for the taking. Our kids won't read much if they have endless opportunities to jump on screens. It's human nature to choose the one that requires less of us—and that is just about always a screen.

Putting screen time into limited parts of the day frees up all kinds of hours for other pursuits—reading, I hope, as well as shooting hoops, riding bikes, crafting, playing board games, doing homework, having long, leisurely conversations, engaging with others, and helping around the house. Keep screens in their place, then, by limiting them to certain hours rather than letting them run rampant all over your child's day.

Our read-aloud sessions aren't likely to look just how we picture them in our most idealistic moments. A pleasant, enjoyable reading lifestyle isn't likely to take shape by accident, either.

But if we set ourselves up for success, we'll stack the odds in favor of our kids growing up to say that some of their most cherished memories are the hours spent reading with their parents.

Keep your read-aloud book handy, peg read-aloud time to a regular part of your day, and get to it as early in the day as possible. Mark your progress, if you're inclined to, and make it *easy* to dive right into read-aloud time by creating a read-aloud shelf where activities are easy to grab. Take advantage of a captive audience in the car whenever you can, and tread carefully when it comes to screens. Remember not to expect your child to choose watermelon over a candy bar.

Now you just need to find a book that will keep everyone engaged. We'll tackle that next.

Chapter 9

BECOME A LITERARY MATCHMAKER

• • • •

> I am almost inclined to set it up as a canon that a children's story which is enjoyed only by children is a bad children's story. The good ones last.
>
> C. S. Lewis, "On Three Ways of Writing for Children"

When my oldest three children were small, I couldn't wait to read middle-grade novels to them. I enjoyed reading picture books, but they weren't the literature that formed me as a reader in my own youth. Books by Beverly Cleary, Roald Dahl, and Lois Lowry were what sparked my own childhood imagination and turned me into a lifelong book lover. I couldn't wait to introduce these favorite stories and characters to my own kids.

In my enthusiasm, I launched into our first middle-grade novel a little prematurely when my oldest kids were about five and three. I decided to start with the gold standard in children's literature, and what other than *Little House in the Big Woods* would do?

We struggled. My kids didn't follow the storyline or the long, descriptive passages. I found myself bored and, in the end, I felt like a failure because here we were, reading our first middle-grade novel—a literary gem, no less—and we were having a miserable time.

What I discovered after that disheartening experience was that not all books are created equal when it comes to reading aloud. I hadn't yet developed my own read-aloud skills well enough to deliver those long, descriptive passages in an interesting way. My girls hadn't had much practice painting pictures in their minds and following along with longer narrative. It ended up being a great disappointment and discouragement to me at a rather critical point in our read-aloud journey.

Laura Ingalls Wilder has, of course, written some of the best children's books ever published, and since that first attempt, we have gone on to read her entire series three times together as a family—mostly through the audio version narrated by Cherry Jones. But there was an important lesson for me in that first failure: some books read aloud better than others, and some books, even if they are read aloud well, are better saved for the future. I also learned that my own delight (or lack thereof) plays an important role in my family's read-aloud life.

• • • •

We want our kids to read because they love to, not just because they can.

We want our kids to read because they love to, not just because they can. We know they won't read much in their free time unless they enjoy the act of reading itself, and so we hope they'll develop a love of books out of sheer delight. That joy, of course, starts with the books themselves. In this chapter, we'll set out with one goal in mind: how to become our own family's literary matchmaker.

THE GOAL OF A LITERARY MATCHMAKER

Listeners to the *What Should I Read Next?* podcast will recognize the idea of literary matchmaking right away. Anne Bogel, the founder and host of the podcast, practices it regularly with her audience.

Anne's method is simple. She asks the show's guest to list a few books they love, one they didn't, and what they have been reading lately. Using that information, she recommends three books the guest would likely enjoy.

What if we became literary matchmakers for our own children? What if they knew they could come to us to find enjoyable books—not what they should read next to improve themselves, graduate to the next reading level, or meet some academic requirement, but what they should read based on their enchantment with the written word? After all, *real* adult readers—the kind who read for pleasure in their own free time, of their own free will—read what brings them joy.

WHERE TO START

When it comes to choosing great books for your family, the first step is simply knowing where to start. You may feel underprepared to choose rich, excellent books. You aren't swimming in free time, either, so pre-reading isn't usually an option.

Shortly after that first reading of *The Read-Aloud Handbook* when Audrey was one, I hoisted her on my hip and descended the long, shallow stairs leading into the public library in the town where we lived. *Today,* I told myself, getting a better grip on the empty library bag and pushing hair out of my eyes with the back of my wrist, *we will get books.* I was full of zeal and determination, growing tired of endless rounds of *Goodnight Moon* and *Mr. Brown Can Moo! Can You?* The library could solve this, I was certain.

I frequented the library often as a child and spent whole afternoons panning the stacks, wondering if it might be possible for me to read every single book in the library's collection. Now I felt out of practice. It had been years since I'd stepped foot in a library. The glass doors slid open. I adjusted Audrey on my hip and breathed in the slightly musty and unmistakable scent of used books.

We made our way to the children's department, where I gazed around the room, eyeing the worn and faded beanbag chairs, low desks with ivory mouses and giant headphones. I saw picture books, chapter books, and front-facing shelves crammed with easy readers. Oversized stuffed versions of Arnold Lobel's fictional Frog and Toad were posed over the front desk, and a cardboard cutout of Junie B. Junes declared boldly, "Reading Rules!"

As I scanned row upon row of picture books, their skinny spines jammed one next to the other on what seemed like a million shelves, it hit me: *I had no idea where to start.*

There are some things you feel you should just *know*, even as a brand-new mother. Standing there at the library, feelings of incompetence and inadequacy washed over me. Audrey squirmed in my arms, and I set her down, feeling my resolve to bring home a library haul fade away.

Surely, I thought, *some of these books are better than others.* When we read together at home, books by Jan Brett or Tomie dePaola left me thoroughly enjoying myself—the cadence of the text and beauty of the illustrations carrying us through each story, leaving us a little happier to be alive at the end of each book.

Then there were the others—the kind I read quickly, skipping entire paragraphs or pages when I could get away with it. They were drudgery to read and bored me to death.

What was the difference? What made one book so engaging and the other so dull? And how would I be able to tell which was which in a sea of choices, unless I had the time and wherewithal to pre-read them?

WHAT IS A GOOD BOOK?

Before we explore the principles of literary matchmaking, let's talk about what a good book is and what it does. You can become a bona fide book maven in your own right if you can learn to look for two important characteristics in the books you encounter.

Good books appeal to all ages

First, a good book appeals to the reader regardless of age. This is the most important thing you should know about good books written for children: they appeal equally to grown-ups. An adult can find herself lost in Narnia as well as any child. And when a parent thinks a book is dumb or trite, there is a good chance that the child hearing the story came to the same conclusion long before.

I remember hearing a mother recount taking her son to the local coffee shop for a read-aloud session of one of the Harry Potter books. They sat at an outdoor table and read as cars rolled by and starlings pecked at the ground. As they were whisked off to Hogwarts, they were joined by a complete stranger, a grown man in a bicycle helmet who had just arrived at the coffee shop for his daily macchiato. As he parked his bike and snapped the lock to the rack, he heard the mother reading.

"Don't mind me," he said to them, smiling and settling in at an adjacent table. "I just want to hear what happens next."

Sara, a *Read-Aloud Revival* podcast listener, said she put on *The Mysterious Howling*, book one of Maryrose Wood's The Incorrigible Children of Ashton Place series, for a long car ride during her family's summer camping trip. "We were having such a good time laughing with the children and guessing at what would happen next that, when we arrived at the campground, we found ourselves wanting to drive just a little bit more," she said. "We kept finding excuses to sneak back into the car—to find the visitor center, to find the little beach farthest away from our campsite." She laughed. "We don't remember much about the campsite itself, but we all remember that story!"

This is what a good book does. It grabs hold of all of us—adults and kids alike—and doesn't let go. It is equally enjoyable no matter our age (not accounting for taste, which we'll discuss in just a moment.)

Good books fill the reader with hope

Second, a good book leaves you more grateful to be alive. You close the final pages of the book a little breathless, a little more in awe of the great and glorious world. The book may be tragic (*Bridge to Terabithia* by Katherine Paterson), moving (*A Single Shard* by Linda Sue Park), or goofy and nonsensical (*The Thirteen Clocks* by James Thurber), yet it leaves you with a feeling you find difficult to express: amazement at the world, an awe for life, a gratitude for humanity and its quirkiness, its messiness, its vitality.

A book that fails to leave the reader with hope has neglected its most important role: to help the reader see the world afresh.

Funny books do it, sad books do it, heartrending or harrowing or lighthearted books do it. They leave us with new vision. They allow us to view the seemingly mundane world around us—and the people in it—with new eyes.

A book should fill us with hope, even in the midst of bone-rattling thrill or heart-wrenching sorrow.

• • • •

A book that fails to leave the reader with hope has neglected its most important role: to help the reader see the world afresh.

BOOKLISTS ARE TRAINING WHEELS

That day in the library, I sat with Audrey on a low plastic chair, reading through a stack of board books someone had left on the kid-sized table. They were boring—not worth bringing home—so I hoisted Audrey onto my hip and headed back to our car empty-handed. I knew what I needed. I needed that booklist at the back of *The Read-Aloud Handbook*.

As you set out to become your family's literary matchmaker, booklists are your training wheels. They are invaluable to the parent who is learning how to put good books into the hands of her children—to spur a love of reading and fill a home with the best books that can be found. Think of a good booklist as a sturdy set of training wheels. It'll help you ride successfully before you can do it on your own. It'll become a trusted companion to steer you in the right direction.

In the third part of this book, you'll find a booklist that I hope will become a trusted companion on your own read-aloud journey. I've read every single book on the list, many of them out loud. But you'll also find wonderful recommendations in books like *Honey for a Child's Heart* and *Give Your Child the World*—books where the authors have done the hard work of pre-reading, thinking through, sorting, categorizing, and eventually recommending.

A good booklist is my love language, and if you're ready for a more nuanced list than the one included here, you can find a collection of all my booklists at ReadAloudRevival.com.

Booklists, of course, are always created by a person with unique literary taste, and you don't want to supplant your own opinions and tastes for a booklist, no matter how reputable it might be. Use booklists as your training wheels, but once you've acquired enough speed and ability to ride on your own, you can rely on your God-given intuition and the 3 Question Test (up next) to decide which books should make it onto your own family's unique list of favorites.

No booklist can be the be-all and end-all, because just as the members of your family are singular and unique, so will your book choices be. Your list should reflect the beautiful quirks, likes, and dislikes of the people in your family.

HOW TO CHOOSE BOOKS WITHOUT A BOOKLIST: THE 3 QUESTION TEST

What if you don't have a booklist handy? Or what if you are trying to decide on a book you haven't seen on any trusted booklist? What to do then?

It's easy to conduct the 3 Question Test. First, flip open the book to the first few pages and read (you'll need to make use of the sample if you're perusing online). Read a few paragraphs (or a few pages if it's a picture book). Now skip to further inside the book—maybe one third or halfway through—and read a few more paragraphs or pages. This shouldn't take you longer than a few minutes—you just want a taste.

Then, quickly answer these three questions:

1. **Images: Can you picture the scene in your mind's eye?**

   What you're looking for is text capable of transporting you inside the story so that you can see it vividly in your own imagination. If the book is illustrated, notice if the images capture you and whether or not you want to look at them just a bit longer than necessary.

2. **Vocabulary: Do the word choices seem rich and varied?**

   Avoid books with overly simplified or dumbed-down language. The best read-alouds contain a wide range of words—the kind of words you *want* to speak out loud.

3. **Curiosity: Are you interested in finding out what happens next?**

   The book probably won't be worth reading if you answer this question with a "no."

A book doesn't need to pass all three questions to qualify as worthwhile reading. Often, it will only pass two of the three questions—and that is usually good enough.

For example, a book containing no text (as in Peggy Rathmann's hilarious wordless picture book, *Goodnight Gorilla,* or Alexandra Day's Carl books) can still pass the test with captivating images and piquing your curiosity. Sometimes a book's vocabulary is simplified to accommodate beginning readers, as in the case of books by Mo Willems or *Sam and Dave Dig a Hole* by Mac Barnett and Jon Klassen. Those books contain rich illustrations and definitely cause readers to wonder what will happen next.

The 3 Question Test isn't fail-proof, but it's an effective and reliable way to decide if a book is worth a place in your family read-aloud pile or in your or your child's TBR stack.

Next time you're poking through the used book sale or clicking through Amazon, put those potential book purchases through the 3 Question Test and see if it doesn't help you make better choices. Remember, we're looking for vivid imagery, rich language, and something that piques your curiosity.

PRINCIPLES FOR LITERARY MATCHMAKING

We've covered the two characteristics of a good book, the value of booklists as training wheels, and how to use the 3 Question Test. There are just a few more helpful principles to keep in mind as you play the part of literary matchmaker for your family.

Know when to ditch the book

Just as we all have a unique palate and preference for certain foods, we also have a unique palate for books. It's okay for your family to love something another book lover you admire doesn't enjoy. Likewise, it's okay to get bored by something your favorite bookish friend positively adores.

Jim Weiss, acclaimed storyteller and narrator of hundreds of audio stories through Greathall Productions, once told me that the first and cardinal rule of storytelling is that you—the storyteller—must love the story too. "The first rule, the unbreakable rule," he said, "is you only tell or read stories aloud that you love yourself. If you try to tell a story you don't like, your kids pick up on that, and it will fall flat."[1]

This is your permission slip, then, to ditch a book that isn't lighting you up. Even if it's on all the booklists. Even if your best friend tells you it's the best book she's ever read. With so many wonderful stories in the world, you want your family's read-aloud time to be marked with warm and pleasant memories, not overshadowed by a sense of obligation and frustration.

I remember ditching *The Hobbit* when I found myself avoiding read-aloud time. It turns out Rob Inglis does a far better job of reading the book on audio anyway, and my kids still received the countless benefits of hearing Tolkien read aloud. I got to move on to reading aloud Lois Lowry's *Number the Stars*, which I had been wanting to do for some time.

I recently tried reading aloud the award-winning book *The Westing Game* by Ellen Raskin to my three oldest kids. The book was interesting and had a compelling plot, but the quantity of characters and frequent scene changes made it difficult to read aloud. One of my kids was frequently lost, interjecting questions constantly just to keep the facts straight in his own mind. I finally realized I was not looking forward to read-aloud time at all, so I let the kids who wanted to finish reading it either read it on their own or listen to the story as an audiobook. For our read-aloud time, we switched to something else.

Several people have named the *Little Britches* series by Ralph Moody as their all-time favorite. I read the entire first book aloud to my kids but found myself counting pages and eyeing my watch through every read-aloud session. When we finished it, I told them if they'd like to read the rest of the series, I'd be happy to get them as audiobooks, but I wouldn't be reading them aloud. I just wasn't enjoying it enough to continue.

We simply won't all love the same books—and isn't it wonderful that we are all made just a bit different from one another? Don't fight this—celebrate it. Ditch what isn't working for your read-aloud time. Delight matters *a lot* when it comes to sharing books with your kids.

Dig around for the right jelly bean

Laura Martin, author of The Edge of Extinction books (which my kids and I find impossible to put down), once said that choosing the right book is like searching for a good jelly bean.[2]

Laura said there's no such thing as a kid who doesn't like reading. She recounted her many experiences as a seventh grade teacher and the thrilling challenge of helping kids who didn't enjoy reading fall in love with books. Often, her students *assumed* that they didn't like reading, but that was only because they hadn't found the right book. It was like tasting a licorice jelly bean and then deciding you don't like jelly beans at all. But licorice is only one flavor. No matter who you are, there's a flavor you'll love. You just need to find the right one.

Don't give up, then. If you're having a frustrating read-aloud experience, it doesn't mean that reading aloud doesn't work for your family. It's just that you haven't found the right book yet. Dig around for a different jelly bean. It's in there somewhere.

Help your child form his/her own reading taste

Bookish people, I'm sorry to say, have an unfortunate tendency toward elitism. I know this because I am a bookish person, and also because I hang out with other bookish sorts.

In the name of helping our children love what is good, true, and beautiful—and in our zealous desire to put quality books into the hands of our children—we have the very unfortunate habit of disparaging books we've decided don't pass muster.

We want to cultivate good taste in literature, yes, but there is a marked difference between good taste and elitism.

It's tempting to tell our kids which books they should or shouldn't like, but good taste is acquired over time. It also varies from person to person. God gave each of us unique taste buds, and because of that we can enjoy rich and varied culinary experiences. I'm convinced that he gave us unique literary taste buds for the same reason.

The best way to help our children develop good literary taste is to put lots and lots of quality books in their path. We fill our home with good books and make it nearly impossible for our kids to avoid them. When we read aloud, we choose books that appeal regardless of age and leave us with an overall sense of hope. We choose books with vivid imagery, rich language, and engaging plots. In this way, we give our families an excellent chance of acquiring good taste over time.

In chapter 7, I told you that my oldest daughter devoured light books when she was younger—books like The Babysitter's Club and Cupcake Diaries. We also read aloud a lot of classics together—Newbery award winners and other books that I knew appealed to a broad range of ages and which would leave us with an overall hope and love for the world and the people in it. She still enjoys reading light books (don't we all?), but her favorites are classics written by Louisa May Alcott, Lucy Maud Montgomery, and Maud Hart Lovelace.

When we fill our children's literary plates with the best books we can find—books that appeal to multiple ages, that leave us feeling more in awe and more grateful than we were before we started reading them, that speak to the human heart through the skilled and lyrical use of words—we spread a feast before them. And what one likes, another may not. That's okay because we have many options.

However, it's important to note that we won't get far when we disparage something our child loves. In fact, we may actually do great damage, making a child wonder what is wrong with them because they like something their mother or father thinks is "garbage," "twaddle," or "dumb." Instead, consider the idea that light books end up being like a small bowl of marshmallows on a table set with a grand assortment of more nourishing foods. They don't take away from the grandness or richness of the greater feast. They are simply a small, delightful part of a wide and varied meal.

I don't feel loved or cared for when someone disparages or insults my favorite things, and I'm quite sure my children don't either. If we want to cultivate good taste in our children, then, we can concentrate on increasing their exposure to good and wonderful books. We allow our children to cultivate their own unique literary taste when we place before them a veritable feast of the best books we can find and then let them develop their own relationship with what they read.

You don't have to get it all in

There isn't any booklist your children must get through by a certain age to be well-read, well-educated, or ready for the world. Might I repeat that? Your kids don't need to read certain books by the time they leave your home. In fact, we don't *want* our kids to read every wonderful book while they are at home. We want to leave some titles for them to discover down the road!

I first encountered G.K. Chesterton's work in my thirties, and what a joy to find, upon reading my first Father Brown mystery, that I had stumbled upon a treasure trove. Likewise, I never read anything by Laura Ingalls Wilder until I was a mother. Those books have shaped the childhoods of countless children, and yet my first introduction to the world of the Ingalls family happened when I was experiencing them with my kids. What fun it was to first experience the world of Laura, her older sister Mary, and younger sisters, Carrie and Grace, alongside my children.

I sometimes recommend books by Natalie Babbitt to friends—adults and children alike. They are often incredulous after reading *Tuck Everlasting* or *The Search for Delicious*. "How had I never read these before?" they wonder. "How is this the first time I've ever read her work?"

When you find yourself worrying that your child hasn't read a certain book or a certain author, don't despair. Don't try to cram it into the schedule. Think to yourself (with delight), *What a joy it will be to stumble across that author or that book or that series down the road.* Fill your child's life with good books, but don't worry about getting to them all. Resist the temptation to assign piles and piles of reading out of fear that your child will miss something important.

Gaps in our children's reading lives make room for our kids to find and delight in literary favorites during their adulthood. We don't want the best reading our children will ever to do to happen all before they turn eighteen, do we? We want them to be readers for life.

● ● ● ●

Gaps in our children's reading lives make room for our kids to find and delight in literary favorites during their adulthood.

Break the rules

Remember your goal. If whatever you're reading is not helping your child love the reading experience—if it's becoming a stumbling block—then change the book. No booklist is gospel.

You, my friend, know your child better than anyone else in the world. And you have been chosen by God to be his or her literary matchmaker, his or her greatest champion, his or her favorite guide. Even if your child doesn't read the literary giants or encounter the best of the classics, he will remember that you read to him. Trust your instincts. You can ditch or skip any book that doesn't seem like a good fit for your family, or re-read a book or series ten times if that's what your family wants to do. You won't love all the books I (or anyone else) recommend, so learn to follow your gut and get comfortable making decisions based on your own unique family personality and dynamic.

Use the concepts in this chapter to help you choose books your whole family will find delightful, insightful, and thought-provoking. At the same time, never let the guidelines set here or anywhere else override your God-given insight and instincts when it comes to catering to the literary palate of your child.

Your goal is for your child to love books and to experience a childhood rich with memories of books shared. Books that delight the whole family, leave them with a sense of hope and awe, and contain vivid imagery, rich language, and an interesting storyline will go a long way toward both.

When you become your child's literary matchmaker, you become their ally, friend, colleague, and mentor all at once. By doing so, you make a meaningful and lasting connection with your child. Literary matchmaking is one of our most important tasks as parents who long to connect with our kids and cultivate their reading lives.

MASTER THE ART OF CONVERSATION

• • • •

> The books are important, but the conversations they started and the bonds they created are what really matter.
>
> Alice Ozma, *The Reading Promise*

Allison set her copy of Shannon Hale's *Princess Academy* down on the kitchen counter and smiled at me. "Finished!"

I smiled back and asked if she liked it.

"Oh, I loved it! It was great!" she said.

I picked up the book and quickly glanced at the back cover. I knew I was going to need to plumb a little deeper to get Allison talking. I didn't really know what to ask, however, so I said, "What did you like so much about it?"

"I don't know," she responded, opening the fridge and taking out a gallon of milk. "Everything, I guess. It was really good."

In hindsight, I realize that by asking her, "Did you like it?" I was inadvertently asking the one question guaranteed to kill any meaningful discussion about a book. It's the question most of us are inclined to ask our kids when they finish a book, but unless we know how to follow up, the question doesn't get us anywhere.

Of all the tools in our parenting toolbox, discussion ends up being one of the most important. Any time we're building a relationship, in fact, discussion is the primary way we get to know and connect with one another.

We've all heard about how important it is for families to eat dinner together. Dr. Anne Fishel, cofounder of The Family Dinner Project, states that dinnertime conversations are important in order to "relax, recharge, laugh, tell stories, and catch up on the day's ups and downs, while developing a sense of who we are as a family." Dinnertime conversation has even been linked to lower rates of substance abuse, teen depression, and higher grade point averages.

When we engage in conversation with our child—when we ask him how his day went, what he's worried about, or what the best part of his week was—we communicate that we are interested in his life and that we have time for him. When we have a conversation with our child about books, then, we communicate that we are interested in what he's reading *and* thinking about. Without saying it outright, we tell him that it is a priority in our own lives to spend unhurried time with him.

Books offer a unique entry into conversation because they contain the best ideas we can possibly encounter. They are, in fact, a gateway to big issues, and we can often enter into a comfortable, leisurely conversation about some of life's hardest topics through the lens of a book. When we read with our kids and then open ourselves up for conversation, we have a unique opportunity to help them encounter great thoughts and ideas, think deeply about them, and allow those ideas and encounters to shape their lives.

This doesn't happen in the kind of conversation I had with

my daughter about *Princess Academy*. Asking a child if she liked a book isn't all that helpful. We need to ask questions that plumb deeper, and this takes time. Like all things that make a positive impact on our parenting, we have to prioritize meaningful conversations. We have to communicate love and interest in our kids, and we do this by carving out a bit of time and space to talk with them about life. The good news? Books make this easy to do, and these conversations can fit into our already busy lives.

HOW TO TALK TO YOUR KIDS ABOUT BOOKS

"When we see a good movie, a good ball game, or great concert—the first thing we want to do afterward is talk about it," Jim Trelease writes. "After my wife and I see a good movie, do you think we rush out to the car, pull napkins out of the glove compartment, and write down the main idea? 'Honey, what do you think was the theme?'"[1]

That would be ludicrous, right? When I finish a book or a movie that I find particularly moving, I have a strong desire to connect with someone else who has experienced the same book or movie. After reading Kathryn Stockett's book *The Help*, I called up my friend and begged her to read it as soon as she could. I was eager to discuss my favorite and least favorite characters, talk through the historical context, and contemplate what the author was trying to say. I wanted to share that encounter.

The experiences that have the deepest, most profound impact on us are meant to be shared. We are communicative creatures, and we naturally desire to exchange ideas when our thoughts and emotions are stirred.

● ● ● ●

The experiences that have the deepest, most profound impact on us are meant to be shared.

Shannon Hale, the author of *Princess Academy*, also wrote a book called *The Goose Girl* (you'll find both of those books in the booklist for teens in chapter 15). The night one of my teen daughters finished it, she found me brushing my teeth in the bathroom, getting ready for bed. She burst in and slapped the book down on the counter. "Read this!" she commanded, a playful fire dancing in her eyes. You can bet she wanted to talk about it. A wonderful reading experience does that to us—it causes us to reach out to others. We don't want to keep our most wonderful and transformative experiences to ourselves.

When my daughter finished *Princess Academy*, I could have had a meaningful conversation with her, even if I didn't know much about literary analysis, wasn't well-versed in how to talk about books, and hadn't even read the book. It comes down to having an easygoing, friendly approach and knowing the right questions to ask.

You can do this without an English degree, CliffsNotes, or literary know-how. If you love your child and are willing to invest time in learning who she is and what she thinks, you can share meaningful and lasting conversation about any book under the sun.

• • • • • • •

> If you love your child and are willing to invest time in learning who she is and what she thinks, you can share meaningful and lasting conversation about any book under the sun.

INTENTIONAL CONVERSATIONS AND ORGANIC CONVERSATIONS

A conversation is, by definition, the "informal exchange of ideas." The best stories lend themselves naturally to this. It's what we do in our grown-up book clubs, after all, and what we do over news clips and movies. When we cut out our favorite Sunday funny and share it with someone we love, or when we get home from vacation and start telling stories about what happened after our car broke down on the side of the highway, we share the story and then start casually swapping thoughts and ideas about it. You already know how to do this—you do it every day without even thinking about it.

Conversations about books don't really need to be that different from any other conversations we have with our kids. It's okay if you don't know what an "exposition" or a "denouement" is when you're talking about books. Silence the old middle school English teacher for now. What we're going for is not the same thing you were shooting for in that English class, anyway. We want our homes to be more like a cozy book club environment and less like a formal classroom experience.

The books that move, shape, and transform us are almost sacred. Isn't a Venn diagram, a literary exposé, or a plot chart the *last* thing you want to do when you fall deeply in love with a book? The best stories naturally cause questions to bubble up within us. They spur more questions than answers and lend themselves to a casual, enjoyable, leisurely conversation. Those conversations can become one of our greatest joys as we build relationships with our kids—*if* we approach them with the right attitude and *if* we ask the right kinds of questions.

Before you start worrying about how you're going to cram these conversations into your already bursting-at-the-seams days, let me share two different approaches for talking about books. You can use either. I use both.

Intentional conversations

A book club conversation is an intentional conversation. Everyone usually reads the book in advance, and the goal of the gathering is to discuss it—that is, to swap ideas with each other.

Intentional conversations with our kids are similar. My kids and I don't have them about every book we read aloud together. We have these intentional conversations only a couple of times a year. The only characteristic that distinguishes an intentional conversation is that I purposefully set aside time for it. I mark it on the calendar. It's an event. I tend to carry out these conversations at restaurants or cafes, if only to seal them in my children's memories as some of our most enjoyable family events.

"Lunch tomorrow at Frank's Diner while we discuss *Jasper and the Riddle of Riley's Mine!*" I'll announce, and everyone will cheer because *pancakes*—and because we enjoy the conversations we have about books. No one knows ahead of time exactly where the conversation will lead, which, it turns out, is half the fun.

The questions you ask in an intentional conversation happen to be the same questions you ask in organic conversations. But we'll get to what those questions are in chapter 11. First, let's talk about the kind of discussions that are not planned ahead or scheduled.

Organic Conversations

In my home, organic conversations happen much more frequently than intentional conversations. We might be on our way to soccer practice or dance class, so I peek in the rearview mirror and casually ask a child, "I saw you finished reading *Fablehaven*. Who do you think was the most courageous person in that story?" or, "About *Brown Girl Dreaming* . . . Do you think that book was like *The Crossover* in any way?"

Organic conversations crop up out of nowhere. They start and end with one question, or mosey on into a lengthy discussion as we drive in the car, wash the dinner dishes, or take an evening walk. Sometimes they last half an hour or more. Often, they last only a few minutes. Either way, they are mini connection points. They help us add one more strand to the glorious tapestry of our relationship with our children, and dive into a story one more time before we set it aside. They are organic because they happen in ordinary, unplanned moments of our day.

When you consider the two different kinds of conversations, intentional and organic, keep in mind that one is not better than the other. They are both excellent tools to use to connect with your kids. Use whichever one fits your circumstances best. If you're on your way to sports practice or casually bebopping around the house, try an organic conversation. If you've just finished reading aloud a book together and want to celebrate, strike up an intentional conversation, and make it an event.

THE IMPORTANCE OF AN EASYGOING, FRIENDLY APPROACH

Regardless of whether you are having an intentional or organic conversation, it is imperative to maintain an easygoing, friendly approach when you talk to your kids about books. We don't want our kids to feel like we are primarily trying to improve or shape them by talking with them about books. Our kids are not our projects. (Even if you *are* trying to improve and shape your kids through stories, work with me here. No one likes to feel as though they are someone else's improvement project.)

You will find that your children open up far more and will

be more comfortable talking about books if you approach them with a casual and kind attitude.

Because being easygoing and friendly isn't necessarily our natural disposition when it comes to interacting with our kids (ahem), it's helpful to keep a few things in mind as we go about this. I call them the 5 Keys of Conversation—and we want to keep these keys in the front of our minds as we set out to have amicable discussions with our kids about books. These keys will help turn down the pressure and remind you that good discussions are, above all else, about enjoying and getting to know your child better.

THE 5 KEYS OF CONVERSATION

Key #1: Don't talk about every book.

Sir Francis Bacon said, "Some books are to be tasted, others to be swallowed, and some few to be chewed and digested."[2] Allow your children to taste, swallow, and chew. You don't need to discuss every book you read aloud or every book your child reads on his or her own. When you demand that every book be discussed, it takes the leisure right out of reading and causes books to lose that all-important pleasure connection. Trust that the book can speak directly to your child, even if you never intervene with a conversation or discussion.

Key #2: There are no right answers. For real.

Remember to be friendly and conversational. Especially if you are having an intentional conversation, you may need to be mindful not to take on a condescending tone. The last thing we should do when we're making a connection with our kids is talk down to them. Relationships simply don't flourish that way.

Even if their answers are not as deep or as impressive as you hoped they would be, there is no need to be overly concerned. There is a journey to Truth, and each of us must make that journey for ourselves. Allow your kids to gradually uncover Truth in all the secret places it hides. This is a marathon, not a sprint. Even if the conversations you have with your kids are not earthshaking, remember that the most important part is demonstrating interest in what is happening in your child's mind. We can't quantify the power of a true connection, and connection is what we're after.

Any time your child gives you a one-word answer, follow up by asking, "Why?" It may take some time before your child trusts that you aren't actually looking for a specific answer or that you aren't quizzing her. Kids who are not used to being asked what they think just for the nature of good conversation—without intention on the part of the adult to shape, change, or grade the child's answer—will probably be a little gun-shy of these questions at first. Press on. Keep asking open-ended questions; keep emphasizing that there isn't a particular answer you're looking for; keep conversing and communicating.

> • • • • • •
> We can't quantify the power of a true connection, and connection is what we're after.

Key #3: Compelling questions matter more than compelling answers.

When you start asking your kids open-ended questions, you may be surprised at their answers. Remember this: the art of asking compelling questions is more important than getting compelling answers. A child who practices asking questions will start to ask them on his own, consciously or subconsciously, whether he articulates it or not. We want to strengthen the child's habit of asking questions and thinking deeply.

Some of the best literary conversations I've had with my kids have been about books my children have read but I have not. I suspect that's because my child knows that I am not looking for right answers—I don't *know* the right answers! I just want to know what they think, and that opens up a beautiful opportunity for connection and communication.

This is true outside of your reading life, as well. You can use these questions for sitcom episodes, movies, comic strips, songs, sports, activities, games—they are all stories, after all. They all have a character who wants something, has to overcome an obstacle, and either succeeds or fails. Try asking these questions about any story you encounter, written or otherwise, and see what conversations erupt.

Key #4: Plant seeds and step aside.

We adults like our truths to be contained in tidy lessons and simple frameworks. But Truth is neither simple nor tidy, and God himself revealed it to us in parables and stories that cause us to ask ourselves questions again and again, to come back over and over again to look, to fall in, to contemplate, and to wonder.

You can't usually wrap up a juicy conversation with a tidy bow. After all, the last thing you want to say is, "and so the lesson from this story is . . ." Let the story be as big and magnanimous as it will. Let it remain shrouded in a bit of mystery.

Sally Lloyd Jones, author of *The Jesus Storybook Bible*, once told me that adults are more comfortable with programs and bullet points because when we use them, we're in control. Stories make us uncomfortable because when we tell them, we *aren't* in control.

"When you read a story to a child," she said, "you're planting the seed. The whole thing about a seed is that you can't see it—it's hidden. Nothing may happen for a very long time, and it's almost none of your business what's happening with the seed. Your job is simply to plant it."[3]

Plant your seeds by reading aloud with your kids. Water those seeds by having open-ended conversations about them. But don't demand that the seed blossom before its time. Your job is to plant and water and nurture. Let the book work its magic on the soul of your child in whatever way God desires. What the seeds grow into—what they become and how they nourish the life of your child—that's a mystery both to us and to them. That is up to the Master Gardener alone.

Key #5: Use simple reading journals to deepen the conversation.

The best questions will often send your child back to the book for the answer. As such, it can be helpful to encourage him to keep a commonplace book or reading journal. A commonplace book or reading journal is simply a place to mark down passages and quotes, to make a list of books you have read, want to read next, or books you loved most. Your child can also include thoughts he has, if he's so inclined. This can be as simple as a spiral-bound notebook, or you can choose to go a bit fancier with nice journals from your local bookshop or paper store.

A child who gets used to making note of language that moves him is a child who learns that language has power. In our home, when we begin to discuss a book, we often find ourselves flipping through our reading journals to find what resonated with us. They don't need to be the most profound passages or most meaningful quotes. Your child doesn't even need to know what the passages mean or why they are significant to him.

Keep this simple, light, and pleasant, free from too many rules or restrictions. A personal collection of book passages that mean something to the individual is a treasure, not something to be graded or criticized. This is not the place to point out your child's sloppy penmanship or poor spelling. It is, rather, one extension of the connection your child is making with the book.

I require my children to log the books they've read in their reading journals, but I resist setting other requirements on the kids' journals whenever possible. You alone can decide what is best for your own kids—just keep in mind that you want the reading journal to be a tool that helps you maintain that easygoing, friendly disposition we're shooting for. Don't succumb to the temptation to make it an assignment, or you may find that the journal doesn't lend itself to reading joy but does the opposite.

When it comes to the impact we can make in our children's lives, we'll be hard-pressed to find a more effective tool than discussion. My hope is that you will strike up both intentional and organic conversations with your kids, and approach them in a warm and pleasant manner by keeping these 5 Keys of Conversation in mind.

You don't have to talk about every book your child reads. There are no "right" answers to open-ended questions about books. It's more important to ask compelling questions than to get compelling answers. Your job is simply to plant the seed, and if it works for your family, you can deepen the conversation by helping your child collect his own favorite passages from books in a simple reading journal.

This will go a long way in connecting you to your child, but it's only the beginning. Now we need to know which questions to ask to get juicy discussions going.

Chapter 11

ASK COMPELLING QUESTIONS

If you have the habit of asking a book questions as you read, you are a better reader than if you do not.

Mortimer J. Adler and Charles Van Doren, *How to Read a Book*

Even if you're able to carve out a little space now and again for intentional conversations and are dedicated to fitting organic conversations into your own family's book club culture, you still need to add one more (very) important piece of the puzzle: compelling questions.

We're not going to chart expositions and denouements—not going to make vocabulary lists and dissect a book's theme in any schoolish manner—so how exactly are we going to talk about books?

It's easier than you might think. When I'm discussing books with my kids, I use ten simple yet compelling questions to get us going.

WHAT MAKES A COMPELLING QUESTION?

In this chapter, we'll tackle ten compelling questions you can ask your child about any book to lead into a great conversation.

Before I share my ten questions with you, though, it's important to know the three qualities that make up a compelling question.

Compelling questions are open-ended

You won't start a meaningful conversation with your child if all you're asking are questions that require no more than a "yes" or "no" in response. You also won't engage in meaningful conversation if you ask questions aimed at assessing your child's reading comprehension. We're building relationships, remember? The art of conversation within relationships means circling 'round ideas—considering, weighing, and comparing one idea with another. We're looking to hook arms with our children, not because we want them to spew out the right answers but because we're curious about how their minds work and about what kind of unique and amazing people they are becoming. We're asking questions because we want to deepen our relationships with them. Make sure the questions you ask your child about books are open-ended. You know a question is open-ended if there is no clear-cut or "right" answer.

Compelling questions can be asked about any book

The questions in this chapter can be asked about any story, from *The Cat in the Hat* to *Frog and Toad*, from *Beezus and Ramona* to *Watership Down* and *A Tale of Two Cities*. In fact, the questions in this chapter can be asked about any story at all, even if it's not contained within the pages of a book. Try asking one of these questions after watching a movie or sporting event. The depth of the conversation will vary depending on the story itself and on the age and development of the child you're engaging with, but the questions themselves don't need to change.

Compelling questions can be used alone or alongside others

I don't usually ask all ten questions when I'm talking with my kids about a book. Often I only ask one. Rarely do I ask more than three. It depends on the amount of time I have to talk with my child, how interested she is in the story, and if I'm being honest, how much coffee is running through my veins. Don't get caught up in using this list of questions like a checklist. You can ask a compelling question all by itself, or if you have the time and desire, you can pair it with another to take the conversation a little deeper.

TEN QUESTIONS

Use the following ten questions to strike up an intentional or organic conversation about books with your kids. While you can stick with these ten questions and have an endless number of great conversations with your kids, that doesn't mean these are the only questions you can ask. Any question that exhibits the three qualities mentioned above is a compelling question and will lead you into meaningful discussion with your children.

You'll notice that all ten questions exhibit those three qualities: they are open-ended, can be asked about a book for any age child, and can be used alone or paired with others. Think of these questions as doors. Opening any one of those doors can lead to a wonderful, meaty discussion. So pick a door—any door—and see where it takes you!

Question #1: What does the character want, and why can't he or she have it?

This question will take you to the heart of a book right away. Every story's main character wants something and can't have it—that's the conflict. Something is inhibiting the character from getting what he or she most desires. There usually isn't only one right answer to this question, and you don't need to know what the "best" answer is before you ask it. You may be startled, in fact, by your child's answer to this question.

One of my own richest book conversations came after I read the picture book *Anatole* with my eight-and ten-year-olds. The story is about a Parisian mouse who is dismayed to discover that humans think poorly of his species. He determines to fix that by contributing something to the human race in exchange for his nightly plundering of the kitchen. After reading the book, I was pretty sure that what Anatole wanted was dignity and respect, and what was keeping him from it was his inability to give back. Basically, I thought it was a book about work ethic. But when I asked my then-ten-year-old daughter what she thought Anatole wanted, she agreed that Anatole wanted dignity and respect, but said people's prejudices about his intentions were holding him back. That opened up a conversation I never saw coming, a conversation far richer and more meaningful than we would have had otherwise.

Some examples:

- What does Little Bear want most, and why can't he have it? (*Little Bear*, Else Holmelund Minarik)
- What does Dorothy Gail want most, and why can't she have it? (*The Wonderful Wizard of Oz*, L. Frank Baum)
- What does Tom Sawyer want most, and why can't he have it? (*The Adventures of Tom Sawyer*, Mark Twain)

Question #2: Should he or she have done that?

Should is an incredibly powerful word—one that must be thought through, reasoned with, and backed up. The answer might seem obvious on the surface, but ask this question once or twice, and you may be surprised at how much fun you can have with it.

I remember the first time I experienced this question in action. I was attending a seminar on teaching writing to children. The leader of the seminar asked attendees whether Edmund should have followed the White Witch in *The Lion, the Witch and the Wardrobe* by C. S. Lewis. We all decided immediately that the answer was an obvious no. The leader suggested that the answer *could* be yes—we wouldn't really know until we followed that trail to see where it led.

Over the next hour, we considered reasons for both why Edmund *should* and why he *should not* have followed the White Witch. We came up with a surprising number of answers for both, and discussed where the story might have led if Edmund had chosen a different path. During the course of that discussion, we weighed Edmund's integrity, courage, and ability (or his lack thereof) to recognize goodness or evil when he was staring it in the face.

As the discussion ended, I was astonished that both arguments had led to the same key understanding of who Edmund was and what purpose he was meant to achieve. No matter which argument we made—whether he *should* or *shouldn't* have followed the White Witch—we always ended up in the same place, at the deeper truth that C. S. Lewis couldn't help but convey through his well-told story.

As the seminar dismissed for a break, I looked at the friend I was sitting with and exclaimed, "So it doesn't even matter if we know the right answer—whether Edmund should or shouldn't have followed the White Witch! Because the truth is the truth is the truth, and it's going to emerge from the story no matter what!"

I was hooked. I knew that the "should" question would be accompanying me on many more reading experiences.

To ask this question, choose any character from the story and any of his or her actions from the book. Ask your child if the character in question should have done the action in question, and then follow that up by asking why.

Some examples:

- Should Goldilocks have entered the bears' cottage? (*The Three Bears*, Paul Galdone*)*
- Should Anne have hit Gilbert over the head with her slate? (*Anne of Green Gables*, L.M. Montgomery)
- Should Sam Gribley have run away? (*My Side of the Mountain*, Jean Craighead George)

Question #3: How is X like Y? Or how is X different from Y?

Everything in the world is like everything else. Everything in the world is also different from everything else. Consider how something is like or different from something else, and you are entering the deep world of metaphor. Metaphors matter because they are how we understand and communicate ideas to one another. When we think carefully about how characters, places, or events in the books we read are similar or different from others, we practice the art of thinking in metaphor.

You can read *Anne of Green Gables* and compare Anne to any of the other characters. How is Anne like Marilla? How are they different? How is Anne like Diana? How are they different? My favorite question to ask is, how is Anne like Rachel Lynde? That one might take your Anne devotees by surprise!

When I asked my own daughter how Anne and Mrs. Lynde were alike, she looked briefly aghast, then paused to consider it. "Well," she decided after a few moments of contemplation, "I guess neither of them is afraid of hurling insults." She paused and thought some more. "They both live in Avonlea, of course. And neither of them understands Marilla very well." There was another pause, then she cried out, "Oh! Oh! Oh! They both are prone to talking too much!"

I bet the next time she reads *Anne of Green Gables* (and it's *Anne*, so of course there will be many next times!), she'll make more connections and think even more deeply about the characters, and of course, about that relationship between Anne and her busybody neighbor in a way she didn't the first time.

How two characters are different is simpler to ascertain than how they are similar. If you find yourself or your kids getting stuck on this one, try asking about differences *before* you tackle similarities.

And don't feel limited to characters, either! You can ask how Winnie-the-Pooh's honey pot is like (or different from) Harry Potter's magic wand, or how Cinderella's glass slippers are like (or different from) Harriet the Spy's notebook. Trust me on this— everything in the world is indeed like everything else. Give this question a whirl, and you'll see what I mean. It's a lot of fun!

Some examples:

- How is Pooh like or different from Piglet? *(Winnie-the-Pooh*, A. A. Milne)
- How is Heather like or different from Picket? *(The Green Ember*, S. D. Smith)
- How is the Trunchbull's house like or different from Miss Honey's cottage? *(Matilda*, Roald Dahl)
- How is the wardrobe that leads to Narnia like or different from the door that leads to the Secret Garden? (*The Lion, the Witch and the Wardrobe*, C. S. Lewis and *The Secret Garden*, Frances Hodgson Burnett)

Question #4: Who is the most _____ in this story?

This may be my favorite question to ask, if only because it is the simplest. Insert any character trait into the blank space. You'll probably need to follow up this question with a second one—something like, "What makes you say that?" or, "Can you give me an example?" If you ask your child who he thinks is the most courageous person in a book, be prepared to follow that up with, "When was the moment he or she showed the most courage?"

One afternoon, after my son finished reading *My Side of the Mountain* by Jean Craighead George, we hopped in the car to go to soccer practice. "So you finished your book today, huh?" I asked, as we backed out of the driveway. "Which character was most courageous?"

Drew smirked. "Well, there's really just *one* character in that book, Mom."

"Right. I forgot," I answered, laughing. "So . . . Sam Gribley, right? What was the most courageous thing Sam did in the book?"

Drew considered for a moment, watching street signs and neighborhood houses pass outside the car window. I expected him to tell me about how Sam—a fourteen-year-old runaway living in the wild on his own—had to forage for food or hunt wild animals. I was certain he'd say something about surviving in the wilderness.

Drew paused for a moment, then responded, "When he ran away from home."

Well now, *that* was not what I was expecting! What followed was a conversation about how it takes courage to set out on your own path. It was much more interesting than I was expecting when I asked the initial question.

If I had led the conversation by asking my son to answer

questions with pat or "correct" answers, we would likely have had a surface-level discussion about the survival techniques described in the book. Instead, we had a meaningful conversation about what it means to step into manhood. That is the power of an open-ended question.

For the record, this is my favorite question to ask my kids about books I haven't read. In fact, I ask who was most courageous so often that one of my teen daughters says she figures out her answer to that question every time she reads because she's sure I'll ask it.

(She thinks she's outwitting me. Don't tell *her* this, but I'm over here fist-pumping on the sly, because what's really happened is that she's developed the habit of asking herself about courage in every book she reads—even when I'm not there, prompting her to do so. *That's a win,* if I do say so myself.)

Here are some character traits to get you started: *ambitious, bold, brave, bright, calm, capable, careful, cautious, charming, considerate, cowardly, creative, dangerous, dauntless, deceptive, disloyal, demanding, determined, faithful, foolish, friendly, generous, grateful, greedy, happy, hard-working, honest, humorous, intelligent, loving, merciful, mysterious, naughty, nervous, noble, obnoxious, persistent, pleasant, proud, reliable, resourceful, restless, sad, selfish, selfless, sharp-witted, sincere, thoughtful, unkind, unselfish, virtuous, wise, witty . . .*

Question #5: What does this story or character remind you of?

Again, we want our children to learn to think in metaphor, because metaphors are how we understand and communicate ideas. This question is practice in noticing how two seemingly different things are similar—and like question #3, this kind of question helps our children learn to think in metaphors.

Answers to this question might be other stories. For example, Chris Van Dusen's picture book *King Hugo's Huge Ego* reminds me of the fable, *The Emperor's New Clothes*. Jasper, the main character of Caroline Starr Rose's *Jasper and the Riddle of Riley's Mine* reminds me of Mark Twain's main character in *The Adventures of Huckleberry Finn*.

Or maybe the book won't remind you of another story at all, but of something in your real life. For example, the impossibly delightful book *The Seven Silly Eaters* by Mary Ann Hoberman and Marla Frazee reminds me of my friend Meghan's happy, lively house. Every time I read it, I think of her. And Tomie dePaola's *Tom* (from his biographical picture book about his grandfather) reminds me of my own beloved Grandpa Curly.

Some examples:

- Who does the dog Carl remind you of? (*Good Dog, Carl,* Alexandra Day)
- Who does Tumtum remind you of? (*Tumtum and Nutmeg,* Emily Bearn)
- What story does *The Tortoise and the Hare* remind you of? (*The Tortoise & the Hare,* Jerry Pinkney)
- What story does *Mary Poppins* remind you of? (*Mary Poppins,* P. L. Travers)
- What story does *Pride and Prejudice* remind you of? (*Pride and Prejudice,* Jane Austen)

Question #6: What is the character most afraid of?

We get right to the heart of a character when we ask what they most desire (as in question #1) and also by asking what they most fear. We learn a lot about a person by taking time to consider their greatest fears. This doesn't have to be the main character—you can ask it about any of the central characters in the story who have their own fears and desires.

R. J. Palacio's book *Wonder* is the story of August (Auggie) Pullman, a ten-year-old boy with a severe facial deformity. Formerly homeschooled, Auggie is sent to school for the first time in sixth grade, where he encounters unkind treatment from classmates.

While discussing the book with my daughter, Allison, we asked the question, "What is Auggie most afraid of?" Allison considered for a few minutes, then said, "He wants to be ordinary." She stopped and thought some more, then corrected her answer, "Well, actually—he *knows* he's ordinary, but he's afraid that no one else will ever be able to see him for who he is because they want him to look like they do."

That second answer led us to consider that perhaps Auggie didn't want to be like everyone else at all (which is what we initially thought) but rather feared he would never be accepted *as he was*, without needing to change in order to be accepted. The fear that you won't be like everyone else is very different from the fear that others won't accept you for who you are.

Asking question #1 (what does the character want most?) could have led us to this same realization. Asking about his fears was just another way in.

Some examples:

- What is Henry Huggins most afraid of? (*Henry Huggins*, Beverly Cleary)
- What is Janner Igiby most afraid of? (*North! Or Be Eaten*, Andrew Peterson)
- What is Corrie ten Boom most afraid of? (*The Hiding Place*, Corrie ten Boom)

Question #7: What would you change about the setting or main character if you were writing this book?

On an episode of the *Read-Aloud Revival* podcast, bestselling author N. D. Wilson said that when he was young, he disliked reading new books. When he was in fifth grade, his dad suggested that as he read, he should determine what he would change if he were the author. N. D. found himself motivated against his will, desiring to make the stories he was reading more interesting than he thought they were.

"If I didn't like a book," N. D. said, "I had to tell my dad what I would do to fix it. That engaged me in a completely different way. I would put myself in the author's chair and think, 'No, don't do that. Take it here. Add pirates. Kill everyone.' I was in fifth grade," he laughed. "I started reading more broadly, and by the sixth grade, I announced to my family, 'This is what I'm going to do. I'm going to write books.'"

And that's exactly what he did. I suspect the playful way his father taught him to approach reading was key in transforming him into the bestselling author he is today. You'll find some of his books recommended in part 3.

You can ask this same question of your own kids, though I'd probably save it for kids over age seven. If your child is an aspiring writer or illustrator, this can be a great way for them to practice. They get the benefit of using someone else's world and characters as they play with language and plot twists.

Some examples:

- What would you change about Wild Island? *(My Father's Dragon*, Ruth Stiles Gannett)
- What would you change about the dystopian community Jonas lives in? (*The Giver*, Lois Lowry)

- What would you change about Grady's character?
  (*The Charlatan's Boy*, Jonathan Rogers)

Question #8: What surprised you most?

We can discover a lot about our kids by finding out what catches them off-guard. Sometimes I surprise *myself* when I answer this question! I don't realize I had a certain expectation until I articulate what I didn't see coming.

I love asking this question of very young kids after reading a picture book. When my oldest three kids were younger, I read aloud *Ox-Cart Man* by Donald Hall and Barbara Cooney and then asked what was most surprising to them. One of my kids immediately said it surprised her how long and hard the family worked before the father set out for Portsmouth Market. That led us on a rabbit trail, and we began reading stacks of books about the lives of settlers during the eighteenth and nineteenth centuries. One question we asked about *Ox-Cart Man* opened up a whole world to us.

Asking what surprised your child is an especially good question after reading picture books, as picture book authors and illustrators often work very hard to surprise their readers. Try asking it after reading something written and illustrated by Jon Klassen, like *I Want My Hat Back*, *This Is Not My Hat*, or *We Found a Hat*. These hilarious books are guaranteed to surprise you on your first read-through and will continue to delight when your kids ask you to read them again and again.

Some examples:

- What surprised you most after the animals got to shore?
  (*The Circus Ship*, Chris Van Dusen)

- What did you expect to happen to Emmy? (*Emmy and the Incredible Shrinking Rat*, Lynne Jonell)
- What caught you off-guard about the people of Manifest? (*Moon Over Manifest*, Clare Vanderpool)

Question #9: Which character most reminds you of yourself?

I love asking authors this question when they are guests on the *Read-Aloud Revival*, but asking it of the reader can lead to a very interesting conversation! Often, we'll see bits of ourselves in various aspects of different characters. Of course, most often we'll relate to the main character, but the conversations that follow this realization can lead to some great discussions and a new understanding of each other.

Seeing ourselves in the books we read can shed a lot of light—not just on the story (although indeed it does), but on our own strengths and weaknesses as we live out our real day-to-day lives.

Jennifer Trafton, the author of the fantasy adventure, *The Rise and Fall of Mount Majestic*, said that of all the characters in her book (and there are many comical characters to choose from!), she is most like Worvil—always worried about that perilous word, *might*. What might *happen*? By seeing her worry through the eyes of a character in a fantastical land, she got a clearer, more objective picture of what's going on inside herself and in the world around her.

Characters in books like *The Rise and Fall of Mount Majestic* pose a fantastic juxtaposition of personalities. Persimmony Smudge longs for glory and adventure, while her mother is mistrustful and wary. The Rumblebumps are playful and carefree, while the leafeaters are impeccably well-mannered. Worvil, the character the author herself associated with so strongly, longs for security and is terrified of the unknown. Throughout the story, it becomes clear how each of these characters' qualities help and hinder them in their quests and adventures.

The tales of A. A. Milne's *Winnie-the-Pooh* do something similar. For a child to ask herself whether she is more like the wary Piglet, kind-hearted Pooh Bear, energetic Tigger, persnickety Rabbit, or pessimistic Eeyore is rather telling! And it can result in a fun and enlightening conversation.

If this question doesn't lead into the conversation you were hoping for, ask your child for examples of things the character did that reminded them of themselves. Remember that any time we send the child back to the text for examples, we're on the right track for digging deeper and opening up a good discussion.

Some examples:

- Which character in *The Rise and Fall of Mount Majestic* is most like you? (*The Rise and Fall of Mount Majestic*, Jennifer Trafton)
- Which character in *Winnie-the-Pooh* is most like you? (*Winnie-the-Pooh*, A. A. Milne)
- Which of the March daughters most reminds you of yourself? (*Little Women*, Louisa May Alcott)

Question #10: What is something you don't want to forget from this book (or from this chapter)?

To answer this question, the reader must recall the story and bring to mind a specific scene. I like to answer this question in my reading journal, even after reading on my own, because it helps me remember details from stories that I would otherwise forget. It's an easier question to answer than "What was your favorite part of the story?" because there's no pressure to find the very best answer. You can simply name any one thing you don't want to forget.

When I read Corrie ten Boom's *The Hiding Place*, I noted the scene wherein Corrie's sister Betsie realizes that if a person can be taught to hate (as the Nazis were taught by Adolf Hitler), then a person can be taught to *love* as well. I thought it was one of the most powerful scenes in the book—and though I might not call it my favorite because it was such a dark time in the life of Corrie and Betsie, it was something I don't ever want to forget. It made me reflect on the fact that even in the face of persecution, we can choose joy and can inspire others to love.

That is a mature example, but this is a great question to ask a small child about a picture book, fairy tale, or nursery rhyme as well. A small child is always ready to tell you about their favorite part of a story.

On the *Read-Aloud Revival* podcast, we end every episode with a segment we call "Let the Kids Speak." Kids call in and leave messages telling about books they've enjoyed and don't want to forget. Kids of all ages leave messages every single day, telling us about the most exciting and memorable parts of some of their favorite books.

One of my favorite messages came from a small boy who said he loved the part of *Five Little Monkeys Jumping on the Bed* by Eileen Christelow when the mama hops on her own bed at the very end and starts jumping on it herself. Of course that's his favorite part! Wouldn't it be yours, too?

Some examples:

- What is something you don't want to forget about this journey around the world? (*How to Make an Apple Pie and See the World*, Marjorie Priceman)

- What is something you don't want to forget about Meg's story? (*A Wrinkle in Time*, Madeleine L'Engle)
- What is something you don't want to forget about *The Boys in the Boat*? (*The Boys in the Boat*, Daniel James Brown)

The conversations you unleash by asking open-ended questions in an easygoing, friendly way are limitless. You may find that one or two questions are your own go-tos, your favorites to ask your kids time and time again. Bookmark this chapter and come back to it often, because a friendly disposition and this collection of open-ended questions are all you need to have meaningful, lasting conversations with your kids about books.

Remember that the habit of asking compelling questions is more important than getting compelling answers. Make asking questions and having conversations as frequent and natural as asking your kids how their day went, or what they did at their friend's house. Don't worry too much about whether their answers are profound. That will come with time and practice. Instead, focus on helping your child develop a habit of asking questions.

By reading with our kids and making time for conversations about what they've read, we're opening doors, encountering ideas, and strengthening our relationships with our children. *This* is how we build a family culture around books. *This* is how we make meaningful and lasting connections with our kids. It is time spent in the very best way, on the most important thing. It is something we will never regret.

PART 3

Meeting Them Where They Are

HOW TO USE CHAPTERS 12–15

The next four chapters of this book are dedicated to helping you navigate the waters of reading aloud with your children based on their current ages. Each chapter covers a specific age group:

Chapter 12: Ages 0–3
Chapter 13: Ages 4–7
Chapter 14: Ages 8–12
Chapter 15: The Teen Years

Within each chapter, you'll become familiar with what reading aloud might look like at that stage and the stumbling blocks you may encounter along the way.

Each chapter also contains a booklist for that age group. I carefully chose books that are likely to give you a positive read-aloud experience with your child, no matter how much reading aloud you've done before (if any). I've read every single book on these lists from cover to cover, and I'm convinced they make excellent read-alouds. This isn't a comprehensive list, of course, but it's a great start for your read-aloud adventures.

HOW MOST PUBLISHERS CATEGORIZE BOOKS

You may notice that my age recommendations often differ from what the publishers of the books themselves recommend. There is reason for that.

Beyond picture books and early readers, publishers typically separate books for children into two main categories: middle-grade and young adult (YA). Publishers choose the category based on a few different criteria, including:

- Difficulty of the book's text (for example, the Lexile measure)
- Age of the main character of the story
- Maturity of the content within the story itself

Middle-grade books are typically designated for kids ages 8–12 or 10 and up. They usually fall into corresponding reading levels, and feature main characters who are 10+. This isn't a hard-and-fast rule (you'll be able to find exceptions), but it's generally true.

YA books are targeted to readers ages 13 to early twenties, feature a main character age 14+, and often contain more mature content, including bad language, violence, and sex. YA titles often (though not always) feature teenage-centric situations or coming-of-age stories, and they often push the limits in terms of content, reflecting what is happening in current culture (or subculture).

I have several bones to pick here. I'll start by saying that while it is a general rule in children's publishing that the main character of a book should be slightly older than the target reader, I have yet to meet a child who insists that the characters in their favorite books be older than they are. Publishers sometimes decide that a book is best fit for 8–12-year-olds primarily because the main character is eleven, and they don't think thirteen-year-olds want to read books about eleven-year-olds. This, of course, isn't true, and the success of Harry Potter in the teen and adult markets should be enough to convince us of that. Plenty of teens have fallen head-over-heels for characters younger than they are. College-age girls still swoon over fourteen-year-old Anne Shirley. Teens love ten-year-old Auggie Pullman from R. J. Palacio's book, *Wonder*. And I know scores of 8–10-year-olds who love books about the kindergartener, Ramona Quimby.

I don't agree with publishers that the age of the protagonist should decide which targeted reader is best suited for it, so I ignore this variable completely when I'm making book recommendations.

You'll notice that I recommend quite a few middle-grade books for teens. That's because I'm looking for something else (not the age of the protagonist) when I recommend books. I'll tell you specifically what I'm looking for in just a moment.

Before I do, let's tackle another issue with the way most books are categorized. Anyone who spends time with children knows there is a big difference between the emotional maturity of an eight-year-old and the emotional maturity of a twelve-year-old. For example, a child who is eight may not be ready to read a story about the horrors of Hitler's era or the Ku Klux Klan. By age twelve, however, many kids are ready to read books about those heavier topics.

There's an even *bigger* emotional difference between a thirteen-year-old and a seventeen-year-old. Categorizing books for older teens (especially those with graphic violence and sexual encounters) alongside books appropriate for thirteen-year-olds is a recipe for disaster for most young teens (and for the parents trying to help them find books to read!).

In general, I find that publishers lean a bit young in what they deem appropriate content for kids. I often find, for example, that books labeled for 8–12-year-olds will be a better fit emotionally for my 13–15-year-olds. In addition, there are plenty of YA books that I'd find troubling to read as an adult, and I don't appreciate them being shelved right next to my thirteen-year-old's favorite fantasy tales.

I'll get down off my soapbox in just a moment (promise!), but knowing how publishers choose age recommendations puts the control back in your corner as you make decisions about which books are a good fit for your family. It's important to know that just because a book is considered appropriate for 8–12-year-olds or for teens doesn't mean it's a good fit for *your* child. It very well may not be.

WHAT I'M LOOKING FOR IN BOOKS I RECOMMEND

In the booklists that follow, I'm aiming to give parents who are reading with their kids a pleasant and memorable experience. That means I'm not trying to find the most challenging books for each age range. I'm looking for books that will give you and your kids a delightful read-aloud experience, regardless of the text's "reading level," the age of the protagonist, or the publisher's age recommendation.

The books listed in the following chapters do exactly what we talked about in chapter 9—they are enjoyable for adults and children alike, they leave the reader with a broad sense of hope and awe, and they pass my 3 Question Test—appealing to our visual sense, using a rich and varied vocabulary, and piquing our interest to make us want to read more.

In creating each booklist, I focused mostly on contemporary books, although you'll find a few classics in there, too. I hope you enjoy dipping into the old standbys, and I've made sure to include a few classics that are particularly well-suited for reading aloud. However, lists of great classics abound online, and in these chapters, I wanted to introduce you to new authors and titles that will delight and surprise you and your kids. You may be surprised that some of your favorites aren't on these lists—in fact, some of *my* own favorites aren't, either! These lists have been curated especially for reading aloud. Some books just read aloud better than others, and I've geared these lists with the goal of a positive read-aloud experience in mind.

You'll find books by diverse authors and illustrators, and books that feature diverse characters. Remember, when we read, we're seeking out windows, mirrors, and sliding glass doors (read chapter 5 for more on that).

I also chose a Bible version (or two) for each age level that I think reads aloud especially well. You can, of course, read aloud whatever translation of the Bible you ordinarily read in your church and/or home, but I have found a few Bible storybooks written for children to be particularly enjoyable and meaningful read-alouds.

Remember, this is not a list of the most important books for your child to read. I had one singular goal in creating each booklist: to help you enjoy reading aloud with your kids. The books on these lists will assist you in doing that.

"I CAN'T BELIEVE SARAH INCLUDED *THAT* BOOK!"

We all have different tastes, so I implore you to follow your own God-given instincts when you're selecting books to read aloud with your kids. Just because a book has made it onto my (or anyone else's) list of recommendations doesn't mean the book is automatically a perfect fit for your own child.

You know your child, your family, and your values better than I do. Feel confident in your own decisions to choose books for your kids—*you're* the best person to help your child learn to love reading and to find books that make a meaningful and lasting impact on her. If you aren't enjoying a book or it's just not a good fit for your family, ditch it and start something new! Remember what we said in chapter 9—sometimes you gotta dig around for the right jelly bean.

More than anything, I hope these books will delight and inspire you. I hope they will lead to wonderful and juicy discussions with your kids, imprint themselves on your family memories, and help you and your children fall a little more in love with stories. I hope they fill you with hope, help you see the world afresh, and grab you by the heart. Above all, I hope they help you love God and love people with all of your heart, soul, mind, and strength.

It's never too late to begin reading aloud. Wherever you are, whatever age your kids might be, *today* is the best day to start reading with your children. So pick a list and jump in. I promise, you won't regret it.

Chapter 12

BOOKS ARE DELICIOUS

Ages 0-3

• • • •

Children are made readers on the laps of their parents.

Emilie Buchwald

A child is never too young for a read-aloud. Babies in utero benefit from hearing the sound of their parents' voices, and tiny newborns are often soothed by the rhythm and cadence of being read or spoken to. Once a baby becomes mobile and starts scooting around on her own, sharing books becomes even more exciting—even if baby seems more interested in playing with or chewing on the books than in looking at the pictures or sitting quietly for a story!

Studies show that babies who are read to as young as six months old have stronger vocabularies and better literacy skills four whole years later (when school typically begins). The academic benefits, then, start when our children are very, very small. We are preparing our smallest babes for future success when we snuggle up and share a story.

But we're interested in a whole lot more than investing in

their future success, right? When we read with our youngest kids, we help them associate books and stories with affection. They connect books with warmth and love. When we pull our young children onto our laps and take the time to read a story, they feel cared for and safe. Helping our kids associate that warm, happy, loved feeling with books is a great gift.

WHERE IT GETS TRICKY

The tricky part about reading to little ones is recognizing that you're successful even when it doesn't look like it. A small child may be babbling, playing, sleeping, or seemingly ignoring you, and you are left wondering if he is even paying attention. How can this possibly make a difference?

Let me assure you it *is* making a difference—the ripple effect of reading with a child under four is astounding. Even if your small child is busy playing with her toys, staring into space, babbling, or otherwise seeming completely uninterested, the language going into her ears is still making a positive impact.

Some of us get frustrated when our child flips the pages of a book too quickly or too slowly. With young kids, it's often an enjoyable experience to simply point at pictures and chat about them. At this stage, sitting with your child one-on-one, taking the time to flip through the pages of a book (even if you don't read the exact words on the page) is beneficial.

When reading with our smallest children, we want to make sure we are respecting them as born persons and honoring their natural affinity for stories. A small child will be naturally drawn to books that are beautiful, funny, simple, and even silly. Remember, good books are stories that parents love to read *and* children love to listen to. This remains true even with our smallest kids.

CHOOSING BOOKS FOR AGES 0–3

When you're choosing books for very young children, keep an eye out for predictable patterns, simple and pleasant text, and illustrations that cause your child to look a little longer than necessary. Kids this age especially enjoy well-written rhymes (Mother Goose, anyone?).

The mark of this age is their love for repetition. You'll find that your child doesn't tire of the same stories nearly as quickly as you do. In fact, it's quite likely that your small child would prefer you to read the same small handful of books multiple times in a row, rather than reading from a more varied stack. You also don't need to have a huge collection of books for your 0–3s. "Prior to age two," Jim Trelease says, "repeated readings of fewer books are better than a huge collection read infrequently."[1] Keep a small basket of a few favorites handy for your child to access easily, and be willing to read them over and over until you can recite them in your sleep.

For kids two and under (or older kids who are still not gentle with books), try both board books and Indestructibles (a brand of hard-to-rip books you can find at your local bookshop or online). Let your very small child chew, sit on, play with, and experiment with books. You want books to become a favorite toy and companion. Don't insist that your small child turn the pages properly. With time (and modeling from you, of course), baby will pick up on the proper care of books, all on her own.

The most important task of reading with a small child is keeping the joy connection alive and healthy. We do this by making reading times warm and cozy, taking our time, and—here's the kicker—reading books more slowly than we may feel naturally inclined to. Let your little ones leisurely pore over illustrations or quickly flip through pages one after another as they feel inclined. By doing so, we let our smallest kids form their own relationships with books.

Any time spent reading with a child age three and under is time well spent. As you are reading those same simple books over and over (and over), you are giving your child an amazing jump start as well a beautiful connection with books, and—most importantly—a special bond with you.

WHAT TODDLERS CAN DO WHILE YOU READ ALOUD

These activities are excellent for toddlers while you read aloud to them, but they are also excellent choices for when you need to keep little ones busy and quiet so you can read to their older siblings.

- Eat snacks. (Try popsicles—they take a long time for small children to eat. Finger foods, when your child is ready for O-shaped cereal or small bits of fruit or cheese, are good choices as well.)
- Put together chunky toddler puzzles.
- Color, using paper taped to the high chair tray along with chunky crayons.
- Build with blocks.
- Play with a basket of favorite toys (it's okay if your child doesn't look like she is paying attention).
- "Paint" with a paintbrush and a small dish of water (to be used in the high chair or outside—tell your kids to "paint the deck" or "paint the table" while you read).

- Model with Play-Doh (when your child is old enough not to eat it).
- Use washable dot markers (found in art or school supply stores, or online) on big sheets of blank paper.

MY FAVORITE BIBLE TO READ ALOUD TO AGES 0–3

The multiple volumes of *Read-Aloud Bible Stories* written by Ella Lindvall and H. Kent Puckett are my very favorite for the youngest set. Simple and bright illustrations tell what the minimal text does not. I love how the illustrations in these books show scenes from unexpected perspectives. The sparse text is pitch-perfect for a read-aloud, and parents reading it may find themselves considering Bible stories in a whole new light. You can find *Read-Aloud Bible Stories* volumes 1–5, plus another volume called *How God Made the World* by the same author/illustrator team.

20 FAVORITE READ-ALOUDS FOR AGES 0–3

When I was building this booklist, I looked for books with a pleasant rhythm and cadence, beautiful illustrations, and a pacing that very small children will appreciate. I tried to choose titles that parents can read again and again without going too crazy. Try to make sure the books you choose reflect a diverse array of cultures and characters—this booklist will help you do that.

Of course, the best books for 0–3s are the books that captivate your child. Start with this list and see where your child's interests lie. And remember the most important part: have fun!

Bee-bim Bop! by Linda Sue Park, illustrated by Ho Baek Lee

A bouncy, rhyming board book, this sing-song story tells of a small child and her mother making a traditional Korean rice dish. Linda Sue Park's pacing is spot-on; the vibrant colors and word pairings in this book make it a delight to read aloud again and again. And you probably will be doing just that, at your child's request! Also try: *Jamberry* by Bruce Degen.

Blue Hat, Green Hat by Sandra Boynton

Sandra Boynton's books will make both you and your young listener giggle—her stories have been described as "serious silliness for all ages." In *Blue Hat, Green Hat*, a confused turkey tries to get dressed. Read this one a few times, and soon your small child will be able to "read" it back to you! Also try: *But Not the Hippopotamus, Barnyard Dance, The Going-to-Bed Book*, and *Happy Hippo, Angry Duck*—all by the same author/illustrator.

Charlie Needs a Cloak by Tomie dePaola

Anything by Tomie dePaola is worth reading, but *Charlie Needs a Cloak* will especially capture the attention of the smallest reader. Poor Charlie the shepherd wears a tattered cloak. Through humorous illustrations and simple, sparse text, watch Charlie shear the sheep, card and spin the wool, dye the cloth, and sew a beautiful, new red cloak. Your children will love to find the mouse stowing away treasures throughout the pages. And don't be surprised if your child erupts in giggles on the last page! Also try: *Pancakes for Breakfast* and *My First Mother Goose* by the same author/illustrator, and *Pelle's New Suit*, a sheep-shearing book written and illustrated by Elsa Beskow.

Dear Zoo by Rod Campbell

Where do you go for the perfect pet? The zoo, of course! But what kind of pet would be just right? Small children love lifting the flaps to reveal the animals in this classic board book. This will be a special favorite for one- and two-year-olds. (I nearly always give it as a baby shower gift.) Also try: *Peek-a Who?* and *Peek-a-Moo!*, both by Nina Laden.

Each Peach Pear Plum by Allan and Janet Ahlberg

A fun combination of Mother Goose and I Spy, this book is one your child won't tire of hearing you read time and time again. Little ones have just as much fun finding the hidden characters in the whimsical artwork as they do listening to the rhymes. My own small children asked me to read this book countless times. I can recite it with my eyes closed! Also try: *Peek-a-Boo* by Allan and Janet Ahlberg.

The Giant Jumperee by Julia Donaldson, illustrated by Helen Oxenbury

Poor rabbit! There's a frightening creature hiding inside his burrow! Rabbit's friends come to his aid, but they, too, are terrified by the booming, mysterious voice. Whatever will they do? Who *is* the Giant Jumperee, and how will they get it out of the burrow? This newer book is destined to become a classic for many years to come. Julia Donaldson is masterful at rhyming text, and the animals' expressions in Helen Oxenbury's illustrations will keep even adults giggling while they read. Also try: *The Gruffalo* and *The Snail and the Whale*, both written by Julia Donaldson and illustrated by Axel Scheffler.

Go, Dog. Go! by P.D. Eastman

There are few delights for a child so certain as the dog party that appears at the end of this book—and the joyful experience of its being there every time you read it. Get the full version in hardcover or paperback, or the (also delightful and far sturdier) abridged version as a board book for the littlest tykes. Rhyming books are particularly enjoyable for small children, as they can help you "read" the book after they've heard it just a few times. This one is a favorite in many homes around the world. Also try: board books by Dr. Seuss, like *One Fish Two Fish Red Fish Blue Fish*, *Hop on Pop*, and *Fox in Socks*.

Good Dog, Carl by Alexandra Day

Wordless books are especially fun to read with small children. You may be surprised at what captures your child's attention as he peeks at the pictures. It takes careful skill and a robust imagination to tell a story completely in pictures, and Alexandra Day exhibits both with her stories about the beloved dog, Carl—baby's best friend. Also try: the rest of the books about Carl by Alexandra Day, like *Carl's Afternoon in the Park*, *Carl's Summer Vacation*, and *Carl's Birthday*, and other wordless books like *Goodnight, Gorilla* by Peggy Rathmann (this one is hilarious!).

Hello Ninja by N. D. Wilson, illustrated by Forrest Dickison

Ready for a laugh? This silly, lighthearted board book walks you through a ninja's day—ninjas, after all, chop, shop, and belly flop. Don't they? But don't wake him up! Ninjas ninja hard all day, and this little ninja needs some rest! Also try: *Blah Blah Black Sheep* by N. D. Wilson and

Forrest Dickison, and both *I'm Grumpy* and *I'm Sunny!* by Jennifer L. Holm and Matthew Holm.

Hush! A Thai Lullaby by Minfong Ho, illustrated by Holly Meade

This sweet nighttime book won a Caldecott for Holly Meade's lovely illustrations. *Lizard, lizard, don't come peeping! Can't you see my baby's sleeping?* Each of the critters threatens to wake baby, and the last page is my favorite! Also try: Marla Frazee's hilarious and endearing *Hush, Little Baby*, a take on the American folk song, and *Twinkle, Twinkle, Little Star* illustrated by Iza Trapani.

Kitten's First Full Moon by Kevin Henkes

All kitten wants is a bowl of milk. But why is that round, white bowl of milk so hard to get to? Animal-loving kids will love this sweet tale of a hungry little kitten and a shining full moon. Illustrated in stunning black and white, this book won the Caldecott Medal for the best-illustrated book of 2015. Also try: *All the World* by Liz Garton Scanlon and Marla Frazee, and *Gossie* by Olivier Dunrea.

The Little Mouse, The Red Ripe Strawberry, and The Big Hungry Bear by Don Wood and Audrey Wood

Little Mouse is thrilled to find a red, ripe strawberry, but how can he protect it from the big, hungry bear? Get this one in its board book edition, and it will hold up to frequent readings. Don and Audrey Wood have paired up on several of my favorite picture books for kids. Also try: *The Napping House*, *The Full Moon at the Napping House*, and *Quick As a Cricket*, all by the same author and illustrator team.

Mr. Gumpy's Outing by John Burningham

The Mr. Gumpy books have been delighting children for decades, and it's no wonder why. In *Mr. Gumpy's Outing*, the animals want to hitch a ride on Mr. Gumpy's boat. And that will be just fine as long as the sheep don't bleat, the rabbit doesn't hop about, and the children don't squabble. But what if they do? My favorite part of the Mr. Gumpy books is the theme that runs through them all: in the end, all will be well (and there's always time for tea!). Also try: *Mr. Gumpy's Motor Car* by the same author, and both *One-Dog Canoe* and *One-Dog Sleigh* by Mary Casanova, illustrated by Ard Hoyt.

Pancakes, Pancakes! by Eric Carle

You can't go wrong with Eric Carle. He's best known for *The Very Hungry Caterpillar*, of course, which is one of the most iconic children's picture books of all time. In *Pancakes, Pancakes!* we follow Jack as he gathers all the ingredients his mother needs to make him a simple pancake for breakfast. The best part of all is the very last step! Also try: *Brown Bear, Brown Bear, What Do You See?*, *The Grouchy Ladybug*, *A House for Hermit Crab*, and *The Very Lonely Firefly*—all illustrated by Eric Carle.

Richard Scarry's Best Mother Goose Ever by Richard Scarry

Mother Goose is always a hit with the very young. There's good reason for it—the repetition and cadence of Mother Goose rhymes are both soothing and stimulating for young children. I'm partial to the Richard Scarry version, though we have several different volumes of Mother Goose floating around our house. Make sure your child has at least one volume to keep for her very own. Also try: *Sylvia Long's*

Mother Goose, *The Real Mother Goose* by Blanche Fisher Wright, *Favorite Nursery Rhymes from Mother Goose* by Scott Gustafson, *Mary Engelbreit's Mother Goose*, *My Very First Mother Goose* by Rosemary Wells and Iona Opie, and *Tomie dePaola's Mother Goose*.

The Snowy Day by Ezra Jack Keats

This was one of my daughter's favorite books for several years. We read it before bed even in the summertime! Peter gets to explore the first snowfall in his city, observing his own footprints and dragging a stick through the bright white mounds. Keats's use of both collage and watercolor are unmistakable and endearing. This book made history in 1963 by being, according to the *Horn Book* magazine, "the very first full-color picture book to feature a small black hero."[2] Also try: *Whistle for Willie* and *Peter's Chair* by the same author/illustrator.

Ten, Nine, Eight by Molly Bang

"Ten small toes all washed and warm, nine soft friends in a quiet room." It's time for bed, but not a moment before we have to go. You and your child will both enjoy the rich illustrations in this Caldecott Honor book, which is perfect to read before bedtime. Also try: *Goodnight Moon* by Margaret Wise Brown, *Peekaboo Morning* by Rachel Isadora, and *Feast for Ten* by Cathryn Falwell (another fun counting book).

The Three Billy Goats Gruff by Paul Galdone

If I could only choose one set of picture books for my kids, I'd choose everything by Paul Galdone. His picture book fables and fairy tales are the best I've found. They are the books that get the most mileage in our home, and when

I need to calm a fussy child, they're my go-to. Do yourself a favor and build a home library of the hardcover editions of these wonderful books. Also try: *The Little Red Hen, Henny Penny, Three Little Kittens, The Three Bears, The Monkey and the Crocodile, The Elves and the Shoemaker, Little Red Riding Hood, The Town Mouse and the Country Mouse, Jack and the Beanstalk,* and *Cinderella,* all retold and illustrated by Paul Galdone.

We're Going on a Bear Hunt by Michael Rosen, illustrated by Helen Oxenbury

Would you be scared if you were going on a bear hunt? What if you kept running into problems? If you can't go over it, can't go under it, and can't go around it, you'll have to go through it. This book is particularly fun to act out, making noises and sounds as you read. Helen Oxenbury is one of my very favorite illustrators for children! Also try: *Ten Little Fingers and Ten Little Toes* by Mem Fox, illustrated by Helen Oxenbury, *So Much!* by Trish Cooke, illustrated by Helen Oxenbury, and *Hand, Hand, Fingers, Thumb* by Al Perkins.

Whose Knees Are These? by Jabari Asim, illustrated by LeUyen Pham

Whose knees are these? Knees like these don't grow on trees. So brown and so strong, to whom do these fine knees belong? Your child will giggle right along with the rollicking text in this delightful board book, and may be able to "read" it back to you after just a few readings. Also try: *Whose Toes Are Those?, Girl of Mine,* and *Boy of Mine* by the same author and illustrator team.

Chapter 13

AGE OF WONDER

Ages 4–7

There is no substitute for books in the life of a child.

Mary Ellen Chase

Read-aloud time gets markedly easier around the time your child hits her fourth birthday. Kids in this age group can usually listen for longer stretches of time. They still enjoy looking at bright and beautiful illustrations but are often also capable of listening to stories without illustrations. Four-to-seven-year-olds are the perfect age for fairy tales and fables, and often delight in a variety of tales from harrowing, heroic adventures to silly, nonsensical stories.

Children in this age bracket will likely (though not always) begin reading instruction. Something you'll want to remember is to keep books a source of delight for your child. Too often, parents and educators are overly anxious to get kids reading on their own, sacrificing a child's enjoyment of books in the process of teaching phonics, decoding, and comprehension. Keep in mind that when it comes to our kids and books, it is not worth it to teach a child to read *earlier* if that means sacrificing their love of reading in the process. Our first and foremost priority is to *nurture a love for books.*

A child with an insatiable appetite for stories will indeed learn to read (though it may not happen on your timetable . . . be patient!). In fact, he or she will be *motivated* to learn to read. And the best part? He or she will still love to do it. Prioritize your child's love of literature, and you'll find that down the road, you have children who can read for themselves, and—even better—who *do* read for themselves . . . even when no one is looking.

• • • •

Prioritize your child's love of literature, and you'll find that down the road you have children who can read for themselves, and—even better—who do . . . even when no one is looking.

In *The Read-Aloud Handbook*, Jim Trelease writes, "Research shows that even when children reach primary grades, repeated picture book reading of the same book (at least three times) increases vocabulary acquisition by 15 to 40%."[1] You know what this means, right? It means we shouldn't set aside picture books!

Too often, we associate picture books with very small children, but as soon as our children are capable of reading and/or listening to chapter-book-length stories, we ditch them. That's a big mistake. Picture books often have a richer and more varied vocabulary than early readers and even middle-grade novels. Continue to read picture books with your child even after he is capable of listening to longer books read aloud.

When you are ready to take on longer narratives, you'll want to keep those read-aloud times short and choose books with fast-moving plots and likable characters. You don't want your child's first experience with longer books to be boring or dull. If you choose engaging first novels to read (this chapter will help you!), your child will be hungry to find out what other wonderful stories wait for her inside the covers of longer books.

When you're choosing books to read aloud with 4–7s, try to avoid easy readers if you can. Easy readers are written with simplified vocabulary for children who are just beginning to read, so they can decode the words for themselves. As such, they often make for boring read-alouds. We want to fill our children's ears with rich and varied vocabulary. You'll find that kind of vocabulary in both picture books and novels, but not usually in the leveled books meant for beginning readers.

In the booklist at the end of this chapter, you'll find my favorite picture book read-alouds for this age group, as well as some excellent first novels to read aloud. Don't rush to get to that novel-reading stage. You can stick with picture books for a good long while before ever reading a single novel! You want the first novel you read together to be delightful and enjoyable, and jumping to that phase too early will make the joy hard to preserve.

At this age, it's easy to become distracted with extension activities that give your child a hands-on experience related to the book. Crafts and other activities based on books are useful if they feed your child's delight of the story, but they are in no way essential. The book is enough—the story can stand on its own. Use extension activities with a light touch, only insofar as you and your child are having fun with them. The goal is for books to become our children's companions, even if we don't extend them with any activities at all. Give your child time and space, and you'll likely see their play organically spring out of the books you read to them. Let planned activities based on books be like sprinkles on a cupcake: nice, but completely unnecessary for the enjoyment of the treat.

Just as in the 0–3 age period, the most important aim of sharing books with 4–7s is to cultivate a deep and abiding love of stories. Every time you read with a child in this age range, you are planting seeds of reading desire. You are creating warm and happy memories that will shape the people they become. And you are helping them understand that reading is truly one of life's greatest delights.

● ● ● ●

Just as in the 0–3 age period, the most important aim of sharing books with 4–7s is to cultivate a deep and abiding love of stories.

WHAT 4–7S CAN DO WHILE YOU READ ALOUD

- Color or draw (pull out some special pencils or markers that are only used for read-aloud time).
- Work on paint-with-water books (there are some great ones by Melissa & Doug).
- Lace cards with string.
- Enjoy special sticker activity books (we like the ones by Usborne).
- Play with shaped magnets (animals, dinosaurs, etc.) and a cookie sheet.
- String pony beads on pipe cleaners.
- Make patterns on geoboards with rubber bands.
- Put together puzzles.
- Finger knit.
- Sculpt with Play-Doh or Model Magic.
- Water Wow! books by Melissa and Doug (reusable paint-with-water books that don't create a big mess)—my little kids love these.

MY FAVORITE BIBLE TO READ
ALOUD TO AGES 4–7

When it comes to reading Bible stories to kids in this age group, my first stop is Sally Lloyd Jones's *The Jesus Storybook Bible: Every Story Whispers His Name*. There is more than meets the eye here. Sally has written every Bible story with a nod to the story beneath—the story that points always to Jesus. I spoke with Sally Lloyd Jones for an episode of the *Read-Aloud Revival* podcast, and she expressed her desire for children to understand that Jesus is at the heart of every story ever told, including (and especially) their own.

20 FAVORITE READ-ALOUDS FOR AGES 4–7

The hardest part of building this booklist was keeping it short! Remember not to rush into reading longer narratives with your child before she's ready. It's better to stay with picture books longer than necessary than to introduce novels too early. And keep in mind that your child is *never* too old for picture books! I read picture books even with my teens. Make sure the books you choose offer a variety of diverse characters and cultures. This booklist will help you with that.

Picture books

Blueberries for Sal by Robert McCloskey
> Once you start reading to your children a lot, you'll begin to notice that some authors' names come up again and again. These are the standbys, the icons, the authors and illustrators who imprint their work on the lives of young children for generation after generation. Robert McCloskey is one such

author. If you happen by a book of his in your wandering through libraries, bookshops, or used book sales, there is only one right thing to do: snatch it up. *Blueberries for Sal* tells the story of a little girl and a bear cub who get mixed up on a berry-picking afternoon. Also try: *One Morning in Maine, Make Way for Ducklings,* and *Time of Wonder,* all by Robert McCloskey.

Building Our House by Jonathan Bean

It's no surprise that young kids love books about construction—this one is my favorite of them all. Based on Jonathan's own family experience (his parents built a house from the ground up when he was young), get a peek at all the stages that go into building a home. Bean's illustrations tell the second layer of the story—solid lines that add a sense of strength and sureness to the book. Kids of all ages (and grown-ups too!) will enjoy poring over this one many times and perusing the photographs at the back of the book from Bean's real-life homebuilding adventures. Also try: *At Night*; *This Is My Home, This Is My School* (a picture book about Jonathan's childhood homeschooling experience); and *Big Snow*, all by the same author/illustrator.

The Circus Ship by Chris Van Dusen

If you read this book to your child, you will spend a good deal of time admiring the menagerie page—it's just sort of magical like that. Here is the story of a ship laden with circus animals. But when the ship begins to sink, the animals swim to safety. What happens when they find themselves in a town full of people, though, is where the fun really begins! Chris Van Dusen says as much in his vibrant illustrations as he does in his text. He's a master of rhyme, and your child will be introduced to several new words in a story that will delight again and again. Also try: *Hattie & Hudson*, *King Hugo's Huge Ego*, *If I Built a Car*, and *Down to the Sea with Mr. Magee*, all by the same author/illustrator.

Daisy Comes Home by Jan Brett

You really can't go wrong with *any* book by Jan Brett—and you'll know them as soon as you see them! Jan Brett's signature lush and detailed illustrations are worthy of long, leisurely enjoyment. The use of foreshadowing in the borders of her carefully researched illustrations is fun even for adults. In *Daisy Comes Home*, Mei Mei has to find one of her hens, Daisy, after she accidentally wanders out into the river. A sweet story of care and adventure, and a peek into beautiful China. Also try: *The Empty Pot* by Demi (another lovely Chinese tale). And don't miss Jan Brett's other wonderful works! My favorites are *The Mitten*, *The Hat*, *Honey . . . Honey . . . Lion!*, *The Turnip*, and *Hedgie's Surprise*. If it's Christmas, be sure to scout out her books *The Wild Christmas Reindeer*, *Gingerbread Christmas*, *The Night Before Christmas*, and *The Three Snow Bears*.

The Gardener by Sarah Stewart, illustrated by David Small

It's the Great Depression, Uncle Jim is grumpy, and Lydia Grace is shipped off to live with him. Lydia worries she'll have nowhere to plant her beloved seeds at her new home in the city. This heartwarming tale speaks volumes about the power of beauty in a world that feels hopeless. The illustrations lend a light, airy, and slightly magical touch to the story. Your children will feel kinship with Lydia, affection for crabby

Uncle Jim, and hope for the future. Also try: *The Library* by the same powerhouse author and illustrator, *The Curious Garden* by Peter Brown, and both *Nobody Likes a Goblin* and *Julia's House for Lost Creatures*, both by Ben Hatke.

How to Make an Apple Pie and See the World by Marjorie Priceman

Making an apple pie is simple, really. All you need is a few of the right ingredients. Head to the shop to get those. If the shop happens to be closed, you can still make your pie—you just need to travel the world to gather up what you need! This book is a fun jaunt around the globe—have a map ready when you're reading so you can find all the places you visit through the story along the way. Don't miss Marjorie Priceman's other, similar book: *How to Make a Cherry Pie and See the U.S.A.*

Last Stop on Market Street by Matt De La Peña, illustrated by Christian Robinson

Winner of the 2016 Newbery Medal for the most distinguished contribution to American literature for children, as well as a slew of other awards. Prepare yourself to be warmed and delighted by this tale of a grandmother and her grandson riding a bus across town after church. CJ is envious of his friends, who are free on Sunday afternoon and don't have to ride the bus with Grandma. But Grandma knows what matters most—and where the beauty in life really lies. One of my newest favorite picture books, this one deserves a place in every home. Also try: *A Chair for My Mother* by Vera B. Williams and *Amazing Grace* by Mary Hoffman, illustrated by Caroline Binch.

The Lion & the Mouse by Jerry Pinkney

Wordless books are not just for the very young! Your 4–7s will enjoy the lush illustrations and rich storyline of Jerry Pinkney's version of this classic fable. This book, set in the African Serengeti, won the Caldecott Medal for the most distinguished American picture book for children in 2010. Don't miss Jerry Pinkney's other fables: *The Three Billy Goats Gruff, The Tortoise and the Hare, Three Little Kittens,* and *Puss in Boots.*

Miss Rumphius by Barbara Cooney

Alice's grandfather was an artist, and when Alice was a young girl, he told her there was something she must do: she must make the world more beautiful. Journey with Alice as she travels the world and eventually lands in a little house by the sea. What will she do to leave the world more beautiful than she found it? The artwork in this book is so gorgeous, it is permanently housed in the Bowdoin College Museum of Art in Maine. Cooney is one of the most talented children's book illustrators of all time. Also try: *Ox-Cart Man* by Donald Hall and *Roxaboxen* by Alice McLerran, both illustrated by Barbara Cooney.

Muncha! Muncha! Muncha! by Candace Fleming, illustrated by G. Brian Karas

Mr. McGreeley has decided to plant a garden. But when bunnies start making nightly visits and eating up his harvest— *Tippy, tippy, tippy, pat! Muncha! Muncha! Muncha!*—he determines to keep those twitch-whiskers from stealing any more of his vegetables. His attempts get more and more comical until he finally succeeds. Or does he? Candace Fleming writes some of the best picture books for reading aloud; her text is lyrical and pitch-perfect, with delightful, enjoyable cadence. Also try other books by Candace Fleming, including *Oh No!* illustrated by Eric Rohmann, and *Boxes for Katje* illustrated by Stacey Dressen-McQueen.

The Seven Silly Eaters by Mary Ann Hoberman, illustrated by Marla Frazee

If pressed, I am likely to name this as my all-time favorite picture book. *The Seven Silly Eaters* tells the story of poor Mrs. Peters, who loves her seven picky little eaters so very much. Most children's book authors will tell you that rhyming text is one of the most difficult art forms to do well, but Mary Ann Hoberman nails it with this delightful story of the Peters family. Marla Frazee's illustrations are hilarious, and as a mother of a houseful of children, this book is welcome comic relief on my most frustrating days. Definitely one to buy for your home library. Also try: *A House Is a House for Me* by Mary Ann Hoberman, illustrated by Betty Fraser, *The Relatives Came* by Cynthia Rylant, illustrated by Stephen Gammell, and *Harriet, You'll Drive Me Wild!* by Mem Fox, illustrated by Marla Frazee. Do your kids love rhyming books? Try Maurice Sendak's *Chicken Soup with Rice: A Book of Months*.

Strega Nona by Tomie dePaola

Meet the book that made Tomie dePaola one of the most iconic children's book creators in history. Strega Nona tends to the residents of her Italian city of Calabria, helping them with their baldness, their warts, even whipping up love potions. But the real magic of this book happens when her helper,

Big Anthony, gets his hands on Strega Nona's pasta pot. Big Anthony is as loveable a character as you can come by—if only he would pay attention! Your child will adore this inspired tale, as well as all of the other books about its characters: *Strega Nona: Her Story, Strega Nona's Magic Lessons, Big Anthony: His Story, Strega Nona Takes a Vacation, Strega Nona's Harvest, Strega Nona's Gift, Strega Nona Meets Her Match*, and absolutely anything else by Tomie. Other favorites in our house include *Nana Upstairs & Nana Downstairs, The Art Lesson, Tony's Bread, The Lady of Guadalupe, The Legend of Old Befana, The Legend of the Poinsettia*, and *The Clown of God*. When it comes to the work of Tomie dePaola, you can never have enough of it on your shelves.

Thundercake by Patricia Polacco

A storm is on its way, and Grandma and her granddaughter are waiting for it by making a Thundercake. But storms can be loud and scary, and will they be able to get all the ingredients they need in time? A story about courage—not the absence of fear, but the willingness to face it—and a sweet tale of a grandparent-grandchild bond, this is a book that will become your standby storm read. In our home, we pull it out at the first sound of thunder. And of course, it lends itself perfectly to whipping up an afternoon snack. Try making the Thundercake recipe listed in the back of the book. The secret ingredient may surprise you! Also try: *Rechenka's Eggs, The Bee Tree*, and *The Keeping Quilt*, all by Patricia Polacco. Another picture book that highlights the special bond between a caring adult and child (in this case, a father and daughter) is the award-winning and absolutely stunning *Owl Moon* by Jane Yolen, illustrated by John Schoenherr.

Tops and Bottoms by Janet Stevens

Bear is lazy as can be, but Rabbit has a plan. He and Bear can partner up—Bear can keep on sleeping as long as Rabbit can plant a garden in Bear's spacious yard. They'll split the harvest fifty-fifty—Bear can even choose which half he wants! A trickster tale with fresh vision, this is a book that will delight and surprise your young readers. The illustrations add their own bit of humor. Also try the trickster tales by Eric A. Kimmel (illustrated by Janet Stevens): *Anansi and the Magic Stick*, *Anansi and the Talking Melon*, and *Anansi and the Moss-Covered Rock*. William Steig's *Dr. De Soto* is another trickster tale (with a twist!) that children seem to love.

Water Can Be . . . by Laura Purdie Salas, illustrated by Violeta Dabija

It might seem impossible to introduce your kids to science through poetry and gorgeous illustration, but Laura Purdie Salas and Violeta Dabija do just that in this lovely book. What can water be? A thirst quencher, a kid drencher, a cloud fluffer, a fire snuffer . . . and a whole lot more. This whole series is just spectacular. Also try: *A Leaf Can Be . . .* and *A Rock Can Be . . .* by the same author and illustrator team.

Novels

A Bear Called Paddington by Michael Bond, illustrated by Peggy Fortnum

One of my favorite books to recommend as a first novel to read aloud, *A Bear Called Paddington* is even better as an audiobook (I love the version narrated by Stephen Fry). All of the *Paddington* books are crammed with hilarious adventures and . . . well . . . misadventures. He's impossible not to love, and your kids will beg you to read just a little more to find out what happens next. All of the books about Paddington Bear are fun, including *More About Paddington*, *Paddington Abroad*, *Paddington Helps Out*, and *Paddington Marches On*. Be sure to look for the unabridged novel versions—these are by far the best. The picture book and abridged readers don't do the stories justice. Also try: *The Tales of Olga da Polga*, written by Michael Bond, about a guinea pig with a wild imagination. Some of the Olga da Polga books, however, are out of print and harder to find.

Anna Hibiscus by Atinuke, illustrated by Lauren Tobia

Anna Hibiscus lives with her entire family in Africa. Amazing Africa. Your children will love hearing the tales of her aunties and uncles, of extravagant Aunt Comfort, and Double and Trouble, Anna's twin brothers. Written by the brilliant Nigerian oral storyteller, Atinuke, who longed to tell the stories of the Africa she knew growing up, these books make perfect first chapter books to read aloud, with lovely illustrations by Lauren Tobia on nearly every page. They can be a little hard to find, but they are worth any effort you make to bring them into your home library! Also try: other books about Anna Hibiscus, including *Hooray for Anna Hibiscus*, *Good Luck Anna Hibiscus*, and others.

Begin by Erin Ulrich and Philip Ulrich

When a young bear named Growly receives a mysterious message, he knows it's time to leave his quiet life in Haven and set out on an adventure. He's got his backpack, a glider, and a whole lot of gumption as he heads out on his journey. The Growly books are wholesome stories that enchant young readers even as they stir a sense of adventure and intrigue. Also try: the rest of the books in the Growly series, including *Widewater*, *Morning*, and the stand-alone book about the village Growly calls home, *Haven*.

My Father's Dragon by Ruth Stiles Gannett, illustrated by Ruth Christian Gannett

This book remains the one I recommend to anyone who is ready to start reading aloud longer narratives with their kids. I've read this book successfully with children as young as three and as old as eight. The narrator tells the story of his father, Elmer Elevator, as a young boy who journeys to Wild Island—where no one comes back alive!—to save a baby dragon who is being treated harshly. Elmer's unusual collection of supplies helps him get out of all sorts of scrapes and escape being eaten by the ferocious animals on the island. The chapters are short, the vocabulary is rich, and the story will keep even your littlest youngsters riveted. A fabulous choice for your first chapter book. Also try: the rest of the series about Elmer Elevator, including *Elmer and the Dragon* and *The Dragons of Blueland*.

Old Mother West Wind by Thornton Burgess

I believe Thornton Burgess to be one of the greatest children's book authors of all time, though his work is often overlooked. He wrote nearly two hundred animals tales for children in the early twentieth century, and much of his work is in the public domain today. You can find inexpensive copies of his books published by Dover Children's Classics. The characters in his books—Jimmy Skunk, Sammy Jay, Bobby Raccoon, Grandfather Frog, and many others, including Old

Mother Westwind and her Merry Little Breezes—appear in his stories time and time again. I love the little bits of true knowledge about the critters that appear in his whimsical tales. Also try: *The Burgess Animal Book for Children*, *The Burgess Bird Book for Children*, *The Burgess Seashore Book for Children*, and all of his *The Adventures of . . .* series.

Tumtum and Nutmeg by Emily Bearn

Mr. Mildew and his motherless children live in a cottage, unknowingly aided by a couple of sweet mice, who help Mr. Mildew tend to his kids. When Aunt Ivy comes for a visit and spots the mice, however, things get interesting. Aunt Ivy is determined to rid the house of mice. This book will make you want to brew a pot of tea and whip up some scones. It's laugh-out-loud funny and incredibly endearing. Don't be intimidated by the size of the book—the pacing and format make it easy to read even to very young children, and delightful sketches are littered throughout the tale. Also try: *The Borrowers* by Mary Norton (for another miniature tale) or *The Wonderful Wizard of Oz* (far better and much less scary than the movie; this is one of my very favorites to read aloud with this age group, and even with older kids).

Chapter 14

THE WORLD EXPANDS

Ages 8-12

• • • •

Reading gives us someplace to go when we have to stay
where we are.

Mason Cooley

Ahhh, 8–12s. I admit, this is my favorite read-aloud age of all.
The books written for this age group are simply fantastic—some
of the best books you'll ever read! In addition, children this
age tend to have a lengthier attention span and, especially if
they're doing something with their hands while you read aloud
(like drawing or watercolor painting), they can listen for quite
a long time.

The most important thing to keep in mind when reading
with 8–12s is simply that you *must* continue to read aloud,
even as your child becomes a proficient reader himself. As
noted in the previous chapter, the increased vocabulary and
academic benefits of reading aloud continue to hold true
through this age group. You can easily read aloud above your
child's independent reading level, since your 8-to-12-year-old

will have a higher listening comprehension level than reading comprehension level.

When choosing books to read aloud with your 8–12s, try to cover a variety of genres. Children of this age often zero in on their favorite types of books and then read narrowly on their own. That's fine! I let my 8–12s read narrowly if those books light them up and nurture their reading desire. I do try to purposefully read aloud from a variety of genres, however, in order to introduce my kids to other books they might not pick up on their own.

This is the age where parents often stop reading aloud to their children, but it's where you actually want to *increase* your read-aloud time, if possible. Kids in this age range are interested in discovering all the things about the world they don't yet know. They have an unquenchable thirst to learn about other people, cultures, and experiences. Demonstrating that books quench this thirst is exactly what we're going for.

When you have conversations about books with 8–12s, you give your child practice at asking questions about a book. What you'll find (although it may take some time, so don't expect it right away) is that your child will begin to ask questions and think deeply about the books she reads on her own. This is because of the way you interact with her when you spend time reading together. You are giving her good mental habits—habits of asking questions and thinking deeply about books. Those habits will spill over to her independent reading and to other areas of her life, as well.

This is a great age to begin reading the classics aloud. Books like *The Wind in the Willows* and *The Secret Garden* are great for 8–12s. Reading classics can be very enjoyable as long as you don't feel the need to be a literary genius yourself. Don't worry about whether you're missing deeper meanings, allusions, or literary devices embedded in the text.

Classics are first and foremost *stories*—stories that have stood the test of time—just enjoy them for what they were meant to be. When you enjoy reading them aloud together (rather than expecting your child to read them on his own), you're removing the intimidation factor. Your child will learn that classics are not something to be afraid of—they are just really good stories with older language. By reading them aloud, your kids get to fall in love with the characters and stories, rather than feeling intimidated by them. This is exactly what we want when it comes to classics!

Don't feel pressured to introduce your kids to classics too early, however. It's better to wait until they are ready to have a pleasant experience than to introduce them too soon and frustrate everyone involved. I've included a few favorite classics on my list, but you'll find mostly newer, more contemporary titles there. I can't wait to introduce you to some of today's best!

Some parents tell me they feel silly reading to their readers, but your children will benefit greatly from you reading aloud to them long past the time when they begin to read independently. You're forming memories they will carry with them into the future.

Remember to keep read-aloud time delightful. Read books that you loved as a child and books that light you up and keep everyone hungry for one more page or one more chapter. It is extremely important that books be associated with delight and enjoyment for your 8–12s. This book list should get you off to a good start. I've chosen some of the most delightful reading experiences I could find. Remember to read genres that you normally wouldn't pick up to see if you (or your child) might find an unexpected interest there, and to read about diverse cultures and characters.

WHAT 8–12S CAN DO WHILE YOU READ ALOUD

- Color, sketch, or draw.
- Paint with watercolors.
- Use Paint by Sticker books (Workman Publishing).
- Sew by hand.
- Knit or crochet.
- Model with clay.
- Sit on an exercise ball.
- Fold laundry (my own favorite!).
- Put together simple kits from the craft store.
- Hearthsong makes design kits that my kids enjoyed at this stage—fairy, equestrian, car design, fashion studio, and interior design have all been good options. Find them at hearthsong.com.

MY FAVORITE BIBLES TO READ ALOUD TO AGES 8–12

Amy Steedman has written a collection called *Read-Aloud Book of Bible Stories*, published in 2012 by Sophia Institute Press, that I absolutely love to read with this age group. When we're reading Bible stories, it's easy to hear the same old story over and over, but Steedman's lyrical language and rich storytelling bring the Bible to life. I think your kids will enjoy hearing these conversational and engaging stories read aloud every bit as much as you'll enjoy reading them.

Another favorite is the *Egermeier's Bible Story Book*, written by Elsie Egermeier, illustrated by Clive Uptton. Stories are told in chronological order. I like to hand this one to my independent readers, but it can also be read aloud enjoyably to kids both older and younger than this age group.

When my oldest kids were twelve, ten, and eight, I read aloud *The Action Bible* by Doug Mauss and Sergio Cariello. This is the Bible in graphic novel form, and your children may prefer to read it on their own. We found the read-aloud experience of it to be quite delightful, however, and the kids were able to follow along while looking at the illustrations over my shoulder. There is also a good audio version available, and my son enjoys listening while he follows along in the text.

20 FAVORITE READ-ALOUDS FOR AGES 8–12

An 8–12 is seeking to expand her view of the world, and the books on this list will help her do just that. What you'll find is a mixture of historical fiction, fantasy, and realistic stories. Some combine all three of those elements.

We still don't want to ditch picture books, as they provide rich vocabulary and engaging storylines that 8–12s still often enjoy. I've included a few favorites for this age range within the list.

A child of 8–12 likes to laugh and be delighted but is also ready to read about characters who are living heroic lives. This, of course, requires dire circumstances and big stakes. You'll find books that touch on issues our children are thinking about— friendship, loyalty, courage, and fear. The books on this list will call your child to consider moments when true heroism is needed and to consider life from a point of view she hasn't experienced. They will also leave you and your child with a sense of hope and awe. I hope they will make you laugh, think, and ponder life's greatest mysteries together as you read.

Picture books

Locomotive by Brian Floca

This Caldecott Medal-winning book is a richly detailed picture book about America's brand-new transcontinental railroad in the late nineteenth century. There's plenty to look at in Floca's illustrations and informative text. Books by Brian Floca are excellent choices for kids in this age range who enjoy nonfiction. Also try: *Moonshot: The Flight of Apollo 11* by Brian Floca and *Finding Winnie: The True Story of the World's Most Famous Bear* by Lindsay Mattick and Sophie Blackall, a beautiful picture book that tells the remarkable true story of the bear who inspired Winnie-the-Pooh.

A Poem for Peter: The Story of Ezra Jack Keats and the Creation of The Snowy Day by Andrea Davis Pinkney, illustrated by Steve Johnson

Ezra Jack Keats made history when he wrote and illustrated the first mainstream picture book to feature an African-American boy. For decades thereafter, young readers would fall in love with Peter, that "brown sugar boy in a blanket of snow." This gorgeous and lyrical account of the groundbreaking work of Ezra Jack Keats just begs to be read aloud. Pinkney's lyrical text slides off the tongue. This is a longer picture book than you might be used to, which makes it especially suitable for a slightly older crowd, and it can provide lots of fodder for good discussions about civil rights and the courage to pursue your dreams. Also try: *The Right Word: Roget and His Thesaurus*, Jen Bryant's picture book biography about Peter Mark Roget and the first thesaurus, illustrated by Melissa Sweet. Another great choice is *Some Writer!: The Story of E. B. White*, a slightly longer illustrated biography about one of the greatest children's storytellers of all time, written and illustrated by Melissa Sweet.

Novels

The Bark of the Bog Owl by Jonathan Rogers

This book has flown to my favorites-of-all-time list. It's the kind of book that's better, I think, if you know little-to-nothing about it in advance. It has all the best traits of an adventure tale with a touch of the fantastical thrown in for good measure. More than meets the eye, this book will make you laugh but also cause you to consider big questions about purpose and calling and what we're made of. This is the first book in the Wilderking Trilogy. Also try: the rest of the Wilderking books, *The Secret of the Swamp King*, and *The Way of the Wilderking*.

Cilla Lee-Jenkins: Future Author Extraordinaire by Susan Tan, illustrated by Dana Wulfekotte

Cilla Lee-Jenkins has got to be one of the most wonderful characters in children's lit. She's also on a tight deadline, because her baby sister is about to be born, and everyone seems preoccupied by that. She needs to hit the bestseller list so her family realizes how *amazing* she is. This fast, hilarious, and touching story will have you cracking up, even as Cilla navigates life as a biracial child in a world that doesn't always understand her. Also try: Melissa Wiley's *The Prairie Thief*, another rollicking and delightful story that is quick to read.

Emmy and the Incredible Shrinking Rat by Lynne Jonell, illustrated by Jonathan Bean

Who can resist a mystery about a very good girl, a talking rat, and a horrible, wicked nanny? This page-turner is laugh-out-loud funny and will keep you and your kids guessing right to the end. The pacing is spot-on. If your kids are hesitant to be read to, try starting here and see if your listeners can resist the pull of *just one more chapter*. Mice and rats play feature parts in some of the best stories for this age group, so also try: *Mrs. Frisby and the Rats of NIMH* by Robert C. O'Brien and *Poppy* by Avi.

Esperanza Rising by Pam Muñoz Ryan

This award-winning book tells the story of Esperanza, a Mexican rancher's daughter whose greatest worry is what to wear to her quinceañera. When tragedy strikes, Esperanaza and her mother must flee to America for refuge. This is an incredibly powerful story of hope, courage, and perseverance. Recall how, in chapter 5, we discussed the importance of books acting as windows, mirrors, and sliding glass doors. This book is a window—one that will open your heart, causing you to pause and consider what it takes to face overwhelming difficulty. It demonstrates that the human spirit can rise up in hope, even in the face of tremendous hardship. Simply beautiful and empowering, I'd read this one with my 11s and 12s (or older). Also try: *The Dreamer* by the same author. Pam Muñoz Ryan is one of my all-time favorite writers for children. Kids who enjoy these books may also enjoy Lois Lowry's historical novel about the Danish resistance of the Nazi occupation, *Number the Stars*.

The Family Under the Bridge by Natalie Savage Carlson, illustrated by Garth Williams

This book won a 1989 Newbery Honor for good reason. Armand, a curmudgeonly tramp living on the streets of Paris, is unhappy to share his space under the bridge with three newly homeless children and their mother. A heartwarming story of transformation, love, loyalty, and family, this is a perfect read-aloud choice for Christmastime. Shorter than many other books on this list, it can be read fairly quickly and will stay with your children long afterward. Also try: *The Bears on Hemlock Mountain* by Alice Dalgliesh (illustrated by Helen Sewell), a story about courage (grown-ups don't always know best!) and *Understood Betsy* by Dorothy Canfield Fisher, a delightful story about what real love looks like.

Frindle by Andrew Clements

If you are brand-new to reading aloud with an 8–12, this is a fantastic place to start. *Frindle* is also a great title to hand to a child who hasn't yet fallen in love with reading. Nick isn't exactly a troublemaker; he just likes to keep things interesting! At school, he learns about the origins of words, and he realizes that he could call a pen anything he wants. How about a *frindle*, for example? What starts out as a simple game turns into a city-wide uproar and pits Nick against his teacher, who tries to end the foolishness that has taken over the whole school and, in time, the entire country. I love handing this book to adults and asking them to read it just for fun. What starts out as a lighthearted read turns out to be a powerful story of a teacher's dedication and a boy's determination. Don't miss it. Also try:

Surviving the Applewhites by Stephanie S. Tolan, the story of an eccentric family's creative homeschool and the boy who desperately needs it. Another delightful choice is *The Secret School* by Avi, in which Ida Bidson must decide if she has what it takes to get an education after her one-room school shuts down.

The Green Ember by S. D. Smith, illustrated by Zach Franzen

This bestselling book is turning a generation of young readers into enthusiasts. After all, what's not to love about rabbits with swords? Meet Heather and Picket, brother and sister rabbits whose lives are turned upside down by a series of overwhelming and disheartening events. A story of courage in the face of insurmountable odds, loyalty in the face of the temptation to hide, and persistence in the face of calamity, this book will awaken the hero's heartbeat in your child. Also try: other books in the series, including *Ember Falls* and *Ember Rising*.

Half Magic by Edward Eager, illustrated by N. M. Bodecker

When a family of children stumble across a magic coin that grants their wishes, but only by half, hilarity and misadventure ensue! Can the children outwit the magic? Eager is clearly inspired by the magically realistic tales of his predecessor, Edith Nesbit. If your kids enjoy this one, try the rest of Eager's tales (*Knight's Castle, Magic By the Lake, The Time Garden, Magic or Not?, The Well-Wishers*, and *Seven-Day Magic*) as well as the work of the inimitable Edith Nesbit. I suggest starting with *Five Children and It* or *The Railway Children*.

Henry and the Chalk Dragon by Jennifer Trafton, illustrated by Benjamin Schipper

It takes a special kind of courage to be an artist. Does Henry Penwhistle have what it takes? First, he draws a dragon with chalk on his door. The adventures begin when his dragon wants to be seen and have a place in the world. But a dragon on the loose causes all kinds of trouble, as you can imagine, and Henry and his schoolmates have to figure out what to do about it. Can true art be hidden? Or is the best answer to let the imagination run wild? Trafton's use of comic depth is masterful. If you love this book, try her other one (another favorite of mine): *The Rise and Fall of Mount Majestic*. Also try books by Kate DiCamillo, one of Jennifer Trafton's favorite authors. My favorites to recommend as read-alouds are *Because of Winn-Dixie* and *The Tale of Desperaux*.

Jasper and the Riddle of Riley's Mine by Caroline Starr Rose

I love every book by Caroline Starr Rose, but this one is my favorite yet. *Jasper and the Riddle of Riley's Mine* tells the story of two boys seeking a better life during the Klondike Gold Rush. A rollicking adventure that unravels a mystery as you turn the pages, this one is bound to keep your 8–12s guessing about what will happen next. Rose's attention to historical accuracy adds depth to the story and may lead your child off on some rabbit trails to learn more about this historical event. Astute readers will notice Rose's subtle nods to *The Adventures of Huckleberry Finn*. Also try: *By the Great Horn Spoon!* by Sid Fleischman, a fantastic story about the California Gold Rush and one of my all-time favorite read-alouds.

The Lion, the Witch and the Wardrobe by C. S. Lewis

I almost didn't include The Chronicles of Narnia on this list because it seemed like a no-brainer. If you are looking for stories that do everything we discussed in the first part of this book—inspire heroic virtue, set our kids up for academic success, and nurture empathy and compassion, look no further than the magical wardrobe that takes you into Narnia. This series has it all, and it can hardly be outdone. There is some contention about the order in which to read these books, but I think it best to read them in the order Lewis wrote them. I recommend beginning with *The Lion, the Witch and the Wardrobe* (chronologically, number two in the series), then proceed through the series in order (*The Horse and His Boy, Prince Caspian, The Voyage of the Dawn Treader, The Silver Chair, The Last Battle*) before circling back to *The Magician's Nephew* at the end, when it can be more fully appreciated in the context of the rest of the story.

Little House in the Big Woods by Laura Ingalls Wilder, illustrated by Garth Williams

Lauded by many as some of the best American books of all time for children, the *Little House* series is based on Laura Ingalls Wilder's real life. They begin in a log cabin on the edge of the Big Woods of Wisconsin and then follow the family as they embark on pioneer life, heading west into unknown territory and facing unpredictable hardships. An American classic, this is a series that will stay with your children long into their adult years. I prefer to listen to these on audio rather than reading them aloud, as the long, descriptive passages can be difficult for some. Listen to the audiobooks, read by Cherry Jones, for a fabulous whole-family experience. Adult insight may be necessary to properly frame the experiences Laura describes with the Native Americans (particularly in relation to Laura's Ma). I suggest reading them in order: *Little House in the Big Woods, Farmer Boy, Little House on the Prairie, On the Banks of Plum Creek, By the Shores of Silver Lake, The Long Winter, Little Town on the Prairie,* and *These Happy Golden Years.* I don't tend to recommend *The First Four Years,* as it was an incomplete tale that is much heavier than the other books in the series. As it was unfinished, I believe it lacks an element of hope that is key to Laura's story as a whole. Keep in mind, too, that *Farmer Boy* can be read out of order, as it tells a separate story of Almanzo Wilder, the man who becomes Laura's husband in later years. *Farmer Boy* is an excellent way to introduce the series to reluctant boys who think the books are just for girls. Also try: *Caddie Woodlawn* by Carol Ryrie Brink and the Fairchild Family series by Rebecca Caudill, starting with *Happy Little Family.*

The Incorrigible Children of Ashton Place: The Mysterious Howling by Maryrose Wood

This first book in the *Incorrigible Children of Ashton Place* series will surprise and delight you as you read it with your kids. You see, the children of Ashton Place aren't ordinary children. They were found in the forest, and it appears they have been raised by wolves. When Miss Penelope Lumley is hired as their nanny, she must curb her desire to teach them Latin and geography to take care of some more . . . shall we say . . . *primal* things. It would help, for example, if the children would stop chasing squirrels. Endless mysteries unfold as the story progresses. Where did these children come from? And whatever will happen next as Miss Lumley tries to civilize them to Lady Constance's satisfaction? A Victorian mystery that is (forgive me) a howling good time. One of my very favorites. Also try: the rest of the series of The Incorrigible Children of Ashton Place, including *The Hidden Gallery, The Unseen Guest, The Interrupted Tale, The Unmapped Sea,* and the final installment (out June 2018), *The Long-Lost Home.* You may also enjoy *Mary Poppins* by P. L. Travers, which will likely surprise you if you've only seen the movie!

The Penderwicks: A Summer Tale of Four Sisters, Two Rabbits, and a Very Interesting Boy by Jeanne Birdsall

Here is the story of four motherless girls who go to a cottage with their endearing father for the summer holidays. We have Rosalind, the oldest (hopelessly romantic) sister; Jane, the bookish one, always crafting stories and getting lost in her imagination; Skye, who does math for fun and lets her temper get her into trouble; and Batty, the smallest. We also have two rabbits, of course, and then there is Jeffrey, the poor lonely boy who lives in Arundel, the beautiful estate on which the girls' summer cottage is situated. Trouble brews when the girls bother the owner of the estate (and Jeffrey's mother), Mrs. Tifton. A summer of misadventures ensues. You'll have a hard time not falling for this National Book Award winner and *New York Times* bestseller. Also try: *Gone-Away Lake* and *Return to Gone-Away* by Elizabeth Enright. Those who love *The Penderwicks* are also likely to enjoy Noel Streatfeild's Shoes series, beginning with *Ballet Shoes.*

Peter Nimble and His Fantastic Eyes by Jonathan Auxier

I told you the story of Jonathan Auxier's year at home learning to fall in love with books in chapter 6. Now you can read his fantastical tale of Peter, the ten-year-old blind orphan who lives a life of thievery. Around the time Peter finds himself in possession of three pairs of magical eyes, he realizes he is being sent on a quest to save people who need him—a quest to travel to the dangerous Vanished Kingdom. This is a tale to quicken the hero's heartbeat in your own child. Also try: The Mysterious Benedict Society series by Trenton Lee Stewart, tales of another boy sent on a mission requiring tremendous resourcefulness and intellectual prowess.

The Search for Delicious by Natalie Babbitt

What is the definition of delicious? Such an innocent question, and yet it sets Gaylen, the King's messenger, on the quest of a lifetime. What one person thinks is delicious is quite different from another, and it's up to Gaylen to find out what definition can really stand on its own. Babbitt writes with a strong sense of fairy tale and fable, without losing the pacing or rhythm of a hard-to-put-down novel. This is my favorite book of hers, but others are equally touching and memorable, including *Tuck Everlasting* (notably sadder than *The Search for Delicious*, but there is a wonderful movie based on it that is well worth watching with your kids). Another recommendation for those who enjoy these books is *The Angel Knew Papa and the Dog* by Douglas Kaine McKelvey.

Stella by Starlight by Sharon Draper

Meet Stella, an ordinary African-American girl living in Bumblebee, North Carolina, during the Depression era. Our story begins the night Stella and her younger brother, Jojo, witness the Ku Klux Klan burning a cross, which changes Stella's life forever. Her town and her life are never the same. Make sure your child is ready to hear about the Klan before launching into this book. There's nothing graphic, but the subject matter is naturally heavy. Draper is a talented story-teller, and this book will leave you and your young readers with much hope, joy, and love for humanity, which demon-strates Draper's storytelling prowess. Also try: *Blue Birds* by Caroline Starr Rose, a historical tale set in a completely different time and place that nonetheless appeals to the spirit of friendship, loyalty, and justice in a similar way.

The Trumpet of the Swan by E. B. White

How does one choose just a single title by E. B. White, one of the finest storytellers of all time? I won't try, so I'll recommend them all. *The Trumpet of the Swan* is my favorite, with well-developed characters, the misadventures of the human boy Sam, the lovable swan Louis, Sam's hilarious and talkative father, and a brass trumpet that has the potential to change everything. A story about the beauty of music, facing obstacles with pluck and determination, freedom, and friendship. Also try: *Charlotte's Web* and *Stuart Little*, both by the same author.

The Vanderbeekers of 141st Street by Karina Yan Glaser

The Vanderbeeker family loves their brownstone home on 141st Street in New York's Harlem. They love everything about it except for one thing: their landlord. The Beiderman is a grumpy recluse who decides not to renew The Vanderbeeker family's lease. The five Vanderbeeker siblings launch a full-blown campaign to change his mind. If your kids enjoy the Penderwick kids (*The Penderwicks* is a recommendation on page 231), they'll love the Vanderbeeker crew, as well. I love books where siblings band together to make life better for their family, especially when those plans go awry! Readers who enjoy big family stories like *The Vanderbeekers of 141st Street* should also try *The Saturdays*, the first book in a series about the lovable Melendy family by Elizabeth Enright and *The Moffats*, the first in a series about the Moffat family by Eleanor Estes.

Where the Mountain Meets the Moon by Grace Lin

Grace Lin masterfully weaves Chinese folklore into this novel about a young girl named Minli, who sets off on an adventurous journey to find the Old Man on the Moon and change her family's poor fortune. Elements of fantasy and folklore intertwine as Minli learns what it means to discover answers to life's most pressing questions. Grace Lin's full-color illustrations are scattered throughout the book, and you'll find yourself hungry for more folklore after finishing it. Also try the rest of Lin's books in this series: *Starry River of the Sky* and *When the Sea Turned to Silver*.

Chapter 15

FINDING MY WAY

The Teen Years

• • • •

Stories are for magic, for grand adventure, for making readers feel and see things, and for taking them to places they've never been.

Gladys Hunt and Barbara Hampton

Parents who read aloud with teens often describe it as a magical experience. You'll likely find yourself enjoying the books you read to this age group every bit as much as your kids enjoy them. You'll also find that connecting with your teens on days that are otherwise fraught with challenges is a lot easier when you've got a book to read together.

Transitions are happening in this stage of a child's life—they aren't home as often, they're beginning to stretch their wings, life is starting to look different, and a whole new season is setting in. Indeed, teens are tiptoeing their way toward adulthood. This makes it an especially poignant time to read aloud with them.

If you haven't been reading aloud much, then you probably don't want to spring it on your teen suddenly. He may feel as though you're treating him like a baby if reading aloud isn't something he's used to. You *can* still begin to read aloud with your teen, though. Hope is not lost! It's never too late to start reading aloud.

A couple of thoughtful strategies can ease you and your teen into a read-aloud lifestyle. One of the most effective ways to transition a teenager into reading aloud is by playing an audiobook in the car. If your child says he doesn't want to listen to that book, tell him you put the book on for YOU, not him. You'll find yourself with a captive audience and an engaging story being read by a skilled narrator. That will be hard to resist, even for a stubborn fourteen-year-old.

●●●●

It's never too late to start reading aloud.

Another tactic is simply to declare that reading aloud is going to be a family activity, much like dinner or family game night. Make sure your whole family is there, then give your teen something to do with his hands while you read. Having something to fidget with can be tremendously helpful for a child who isn't used to listening to a story being read aloud. Playing an audiobook at mealtimes or on a lazy Saturday while you gather in the family room is another way to ease in.

Here's the biggest thing to remember: our teens don't want to be our "projects." If they sense that we are reading aloud to them in order to *improve* them, then they will resist (I mean, wouldn't you?). If, however, they sense that we are listening to a story or reading aloud for our own delight and enjoyment, they may find the whole experience a bit more palatable.

Your teen wants to be treated like an adult reader because (heads up!) he *is* just about an adult! So go out of your way to treat your child like you're both readers on a journey together. Pay special attention to chapter 6 on creating a book club culture in your home. Avoid being condescending about your teen's book · choices or disparaging the frequency (or infrequency) with which they read.

Even reading a single book together each year will stick with your child when he leaves home. And since your child is likely leaving home in the not-too-distant future, it's a time investment well worth making while you still have the opportunity. Focus less on quantity and more on making it normal to read and talk about books together. This is a preview for future interactions about books. You are paving the way for changes that are happening in your relationship as your child transitions into young adulthood.

Conversations are where the bonding happens with teens (and probably every age, actually). Don't skimp here. Read less together if it means you're making time to talk more. Talk, talk, talk. Let books be your springboard for nurturing a personal relationship with your teen.

There is still value in sophisticated language patterns coming in through the ear at this phase, and audiobooks can be a wonderful way to make that happen. A teen can listen to audiobooks on a drive to work, a jog for cross-country training, or during a bus ride. If you're listening to the same audiobook (at a different time or place), you can still grab a latte together and talk about it later, using the conversation starters found in chapter 11 of this book. The story you share bridges you and your teen, even when life is busy and starts looking different than it has before.

Focus less on reading the "right" books. The most important thing is that you nurture a love of the written word and an appreciation for stories in your teen—and that you communicate how much you enjoy spending time with him. By sharing books, we can help our teens find their way in this crazy, mixed-up world.

WHAT TEENS CAN DO WHILE YOU READ ALOUD

- Knit or crochet.
- Make models (airplanes, etc.).
- Practice calligraphy or hand lettering.
- Draw or sketch.
- Paint with watercolors.
- Model with clay.
- Do chores (wash dishes, fold laundry, bake, cook, etc.).
- Make a collage.

MY FAVORITE BIBLE TO READ ALOUD TO TEENS

During the teen years, I prefer to read aloud from whatever Bible translation the adults at our house are reading. My own favorite is *The Ignatius Bible* (RSV), but you can read the NIV, KJV, NAB, or any other translation used at your church or in your home. *The Message* can be a nice change of pace for a read-aloud, even if you don't usually use it in your home. Review the principles from chapter 10 of this book on the art of conversation to remind yourself not to get in the way when your child meets a story from Scripture. It's important that we don't turn Bible reading into didactic teaching sessions when there is so much potential for a story to meet our children on a deep and lasting level just the way it is.

20 FAVORITE READ-ALOUDS FOR TEENS

Teens are ready to tackle bigger, meatier subject matter and more complicated text, but that doesn't mean they always want to! What you'll find on this list is a mix—some books are light and fun, other selections are heavy and important. Many selections are both.

All of the titles, I think, lend themselves well to reading aloud and being shared. Be sure to read the descriptions, as some of these selections are better suited for older teens.

You'll find that my recommendations for teens include a fair number of middle-grade books, some adult selections, and just a few YA titles. I've tried to avoid books that contain prolific bad language, graphic violence, and sexual encounters. Even if you are comfortable handing your teens books that contain such content, you probably don't want to read them *aloud* (ask me how I know). There are a couple of exceptions, and I mention those in the book descriptions. But mainly, I've chosen books that will cultivate a warm and memorable family experience.

I'm including a few picture book selections as well, and you might be surprised at how meaningful these can be to read with teens. The picture books on this list have more complicated or weighty content than the books I've suggested you read aloud with younger kids in the previous chapters. When you're crunched for time or wary about committing to reading a longer book with your teen, choose one of these picture books to read aloud—that will give you a quick win.

Remember, as always, to give your child the opportunity to meet characters and settings different from the ones they are used to. Provide books written by diverse authors and stories about diverse characters in situations unlike your child's day-to-day life. This booklist will give you a good start in that direction. Most of all, remember that reading with teens is first and foremost about creating connections that will last long past the time they leave home. Have fun and enjoy your teenager!

Picture books

Castle by David Macaulay

Heralded as an Explainer-in-Chief, Macaulay is perhaps one of the most talented pen-and-ink illustrators today. These are no ordinary picture books. *Castle* is his most well-known title, but he has also penned others. If your child tends to prefer nonfiction, this is a great place to start for a read-aloud. While Macaulay (schooled in architecture before he began making books for children) tells stories of buildings, what he's really doing is telling stories of people. Also try: David Macaulay's other works, including *Cathedral*, *City*, *Pyramid*, *The Way Things Work Now*, and others. While he's best known for his pen-and-ink illustrations, you can also find delightful versions of many of his books in color.

Pink and Say by Patricia Polacco

This book will convince you that picture books are not just for little kids. *Pink and Say* is the gorgeous story of two Civil War heroes—one African-American, one white—and their unlikely friendship on an American battlefield. It's a story you won't soon forget—a remarkable tale of mercy, kindness, heartbreak, and hope. If this one hits the spot, also try: *The Butterfly* by Patricia Polacco, which tells the story of two young girls in a French village that has been invaded by Nazi troops during World War II. More beautiful picture book choices tackling weighty topics include *Show Way* by Jacqueline Woodson, illustrated by Hudson Talbott (slavery) and *Sit-In* by Andrea Pinkney, illustrated by Brian Pinkney (the civil rights movement).

Novels and longer nonfiction

The Boys in the Boat: Nine Americans and Their Epic Quest for Gold at the 1936 Berlin Olympics by Daniel James Brown

You can read the original version with teens, but if you're intimidated by the book's length, then go for the Young Readers Adaptation—I don't think you'll be disappointed. The original version of the book gives more historical detail and background, but the Young Readers Adaptation is extremely well-done. In this book you'll encounter the true story of Joe Rantz, a boy who suffered mightily during his childhood but rose up to grab life by its horns anyway. This is a story teen athletes especially will enjoy. Also try: *God's Smuggler* by Brother Andrew, the true story of a boy who lost his way and then found it working undercover for God, smuggling Bibles behind the borders of closed nations. I was surprised by how much of a page-turner this book turned out to be.

Brown Girl Dreaming by Jacqueline Woodson

As this is a novel in verse, you could read each poem individually. When you read them in order from front to back, however, they tell the story of Jacqueline's childhood as an African-American girl growing up in both Ohio and South Carolina during and just after the civil rights movement. It's the kind of book that leaves you aching and grateful and full of hope, all at once. You can read this one aloud (I read it aloud to myself!) or listen to Jacqueline Woodson herself narrate it as an audiobook. Also try: Renée Watson's *Piecing Me Together*, the story of a black teenage girl who is trying to make her way in a world that doesn't make it easy.

Bud, Not Buddy by Christopher Paul Curtis

Ten-year old Bud is on the lam. He's run away from the orphan home and from the terrible Amos family in search of his father and a better future. But times are hard in Flint, Michigan in 1936, and Bud (not Buddy) has it tough trying to make his way. His momma only left him one measly clue to finding his father: the flyers she treasured, featuring Herman E. Calloway and his band, the Dusky Devastators of the Depression!!!!!! (That's six exclamation points, so you *know* the band is popular.) I read this book aloud to my teens, and I don't know that we've ever laughed so hard. It's a story that will break your heart and then put it back together. If you like this one, also try other books by Christopher Paul Curtis, particularly *The Watsons Go to Birmingham—1963*.

The Charlatan's Boy by Jonathan Rogers

Welcome to Corenwald (or welcome back, if you've read the Wilderking Trilogy, which I recommend in chapter 14). In this story, you'll meet an ugly boy named Grady and the circus huckster Floyd as they tramp through villages tricking folks into falling for their mythical feechie act. When business slows, Floyd drums up a grand scheme that has some surprising results for both the people in Corenwald and for Grady himself. This is a book about knowing who you are and (more importantly) knowing *whose* you are. Lots to enjoy and talk about—you might even find yourself staying up late at night to read ahead, just to see how it all turns out. Also try: *The Screwtape Letters* by C. S. Lewis, a classic that will have you contemplating big ideas from a unique perspective. I actually re-read *The Screwtape Letters* every year (it's *that* good!). And of course, fans of both Rogers and Lewis will likely also be fans of J.R.R. Tolkien's *The Hobbit*, as well as The Lord of the Rings books, including *The Fellowship of the Ring*, *The Two Towers*, and *The Return of the King*. We prefer to listen to *The Lord of the Rings* audiobooks narrated by Rob Inglis.

Echo by Pam Muñoz Ryan

Don't read this book—listen to it. The audiobook narrated by Mark Bramhall, David de Vries, Andrews MacLeod, and Rebecca Soler is an exquisite experience. The book begins with the fairy-tale-like story of Otto, three sisters, and a harmonica. Decades later, we meet the harmonica again in the hands of Friedrich, a German boy on the wrong side of the Nazi Party during World War II. A few years later, in Pennsylvania, the harmonica falls into the hands of an orphan named Mike and his brother Frankie, who dream of having a family of their own. Then we meet Ivy Lopez, a girl in California during the 1940s who struggles to fight for her American identity in a time of cultural turmoil, and of course, the harmonica finds its way into her hands. The author weaves the threads of these stories together in a truly magical masterpiece. This is one of my favorite books of all time. Highly, highly recommended. Also try: other works by Pam Muñoz Ryan (you'll find descriptions for both *The Dreamer* and *Esperanza Rising* in chapter 14). You also may enjoy the mix of historical fiction, imagination, and folklore in Kenneth Oppel's book (illustrated by Jim Tierney), *The Boundless*, about a boy who longs for adventure—and finds it!—on the Canadian Railway.

Fever 1793 by Laurie Halse Anderson

It's summer during the late eighteenth century in Philadelphia, and Mattie Cook is caught in the middle of a plague that sweeps the city and destroys everything in its path. When her mother becomes gravely ill, Mattie and her grandfather seek healthier air in the country, but soon discover the yellow fever can't be outrun. Based on the true events of the yellow fever epidemic of 1793, this page-turning historical novel will keep you and your teen on the edge of your seats. If you want to learn more about the Epidemic, also try Jim Murphy's *An American Plague: The True and Terrifying Story of the Yellow Fever Epidemic of 1793* (a Newbery Honor book that shares actual accounts and true artifacts from history).

The Giver by Lois Lowry

In this book, we meet twelve-year-old Jonas, a boy who lives in a placid world of "ideal" control and conformity. Jonas is assigned the role of Receiver of Memory and begins to uncover the dark underbelly of his "perfect" world. Perhaps the original dystopian novel for young adults, *The Giver* is a haunting story that will provide you and your teens with much to discuss. Also try: the rest of the Giver Quartet, including *Gathering Blue*, *Messenger*, and *Son*, all by the startlingly talented Lois Lowry. Teens who enjoy dystopian fiction may also enjoy The Hunger Games series by Suzanne Collins. The Hunger Games can serve as a catalyst for conversations with your teens about big and relevant social issues if you make time to discuss the series after reading it.

The Goose Girl by Shannon Hale

This is the first in the Books of Bayern series, and it's a retelling of Grimm's fairy tale by the same name. Excellent writing and the well-paced plot will reel in your teens right from the start—and this one isn't just for girls! There's plenty of adventure, romance, and hand-to-hand combat to keep everyone engaged. Also try: the rest of the Books of Bayern, including *Enna Burning*, *River Secrets*, and *Forest Born*. Teens will also enjoy *Princess Academy*—deeper and richer than its title sounds, and suitable for a younger audience than the Books of Bayern.

Hattie Big Sky by Kirby Larson

Hattie Here-and-There has taken on a formidable task—to prove up her late uncle's Montana claim all on her own. This historical novel will take you to the American frontier with a girl who faces the harsh natural world in order to find out what it really means to be "home." It won a Newbery Honor in 2008 and is followed by a wonderful sequel, *Hattie Ever After*, as the main character continues her quest to make her way "home" by moving to San Francisco to pursue her dream of becoming a reporter. If your teen enjoys these books about Hattie, also try the adult novel by Susan Meissner, *A Fall of Marigolds*. In *A Fall of Marigolds*, Meissner weaves together two tales: one of Clara Wood, who must sort out her world after the catastrophic Triangle Shirtwaist Fire of Manhattan in 1911, and the other of Taryn Michaels, who is rebuilding her life after losing her husband in the 9/11 attack on the World Trade Center. Teens who enjoy historical fiction like *Hattie Big Sky* and *Hattie Ever*

After may also enjoy *The True Confessions of Charlotte Doyle*, a 19th-century tale about a thirteen-year-old girl's harrowing journey across the Atlantic.

The Hiding Place by Corrie ten Boom

This is the incredibly moving and true story of Corrie ten Boom, a watchmaker who was thrust into the Dutch resistance during World War II. I think it's best read with older teens, as it will undoubtedly shatter your heart as you read the startling and terrifying account of life in a Nazi prison camp. I think it's best to read this one *aloud* with your teen (rather than having them read it on their own) so that you can talk through the complicated and heartrending facts of this terrible time in history. This book doesn't leave the reader in despair, though. Like all truly wonderful books, you close the last page with a promise of hope and goodwill—one your teen will be thinking about for years to come. Highly recommended. Also try: *Unbroken: An Olympian's Journey from Airman to Castaway to Captive*. This book describes the violent horrors of prison camps in more detail than *The Hiding Place*, so save it for your oldest teens and make sure to set aside lots of time to help your teen talk through and process the book. Note: I recommend the Young Adult Adaptation of this book.

Homeless Bird by Gloria Whelan

In this historical novel set in India, master storyteller Gloria Whelan writes the story of Koly, a thirteen-year-old girl who must leave her childhood home to face an arranged marriage. After the ceremony is complete, however, Koly learns that her future has been traded for a dowry, and in an unfortunate turn of events, her life changes abruptly. Cast out from society and abandoned by everyone she has ever known, Koly must learn to make her own way and find beauty and happiness in her unlucky circumstances. Also try: other books by Gloria Whelan, especially the achingly beautiful and moving *Listening for Lions*. Teens who enjoy *Homeless Bird* may also enjoy the book by Ji-li Jiang, *Red Scarf Girl: A Memoir of the Cultural Revolution*, about growing up in China under communist revolutionary Mao Zedong.

Inside Out and Back Again by Thanhha Lai

You'll find this one in the middle-grade section of the library or bookstore, but don't let that fool you—my teen and I enjoyed it every bit as much as a twelve-year-old might. In this verse novel, you'll meet Hà, a girl whose family flees Vietnam after the Fall of Saigon. Her experience as a young immigrant to America is touching and poignant. This book has won several awards, including a Newbery Honor and a National Book Award. If you enjoy this novel, also try other novels in verse: *The Crossover* by Kwame Alexander (especially suitable for your teen boys and/or athletes) and *Out of the Dust* by Karen Hesse, a startling story set in the Dust Bowl during the Depression.

Moon Over Manifest by Clare Vanderpool

This book won the Newbery Medal for excellence in children's literature in 2011. Abilene Tucker's father sends her to the immigrant town of Manifest in rural Kansas with little explanation, and Abilene feels abandoned and alone. In her room, she discovers a hidden cigar box full of mementos, which leads her to unravel stories of Manifest and the people who live there. It's a story of loss, belonging, home, and forgiveness, told in an unforgettably beautiful way. Also try: *Navigating Early* by Clare Vanderpool. I think Clare Vanderpool is one of today's most talented writers.

Okay for Now by Gary D. Schmidt

Gary D. Schmidt has written some of the most compelling novels I've ever read, and this is my favorite of them all. It's a book that will make you want to stare at Audubon paintings, read *Jane Eyre*, thank a veteran, get an orchid, and hug a mean kid. The main character is Doug Swietek, a "skinny thug" who suffers at the hands of an abusive father. Doug must navigate his tumultuous home life, his struggles in school, and an older brother who returns from Vietnam profoundly scarred and disabled. Schmidt's writing style will change the way you see the world and the people who are hurting all around you. This is one of my very top picks. If you're only going to read a couple of books with your teen, make sure this is one of them. Also try: *The Wednesday Wars* by Gary Schmidt. It actually takes place before *Okay for Now*, but you can read them in any order. What Schmidt does for Audubon in *Okay for Now* (that is, light you on fire to find out more about his work) he does for Shakespeare in *The Wednesday Wars*.

On the Edge of the Dark Sea of Darkness by Andrew Peterson

This is the first tale in the Wingfeather Saga, a series I mention frequently throughout this book. The saga tells the story of the Igiby family: Janner, Tink, and Leeli, their dog Nugget, devoted mother Nia, and ex-pirate grandfather, Podo Helmer. They live in Glipwood, a town overtaken by the evil and ferocious Fangs of Dang. Fans of Tolkien and Lewis will especially appreciate the extraordinary creatures and fascinating characters that cross paths with the Igiby children as they uncover their true identity and learn what it means to be who they are. More than meets the eye, these aren't just fantasy adventures. They are tales that speak to what it costs to answer the call we have been created for. Also try: the rest of the series in the Wingfeather Saga. Book two is *North! Or Be Eaten* and is followed by *The Monster in the Hollows* and *The Warden and the Wolf King.* You may also enjoy *Wingfeather Tales,* a collection of short stories about the creatures and characters of Glipwood. These books can be read with younger kids (about age 9+), as well.

A Single Shard by Linda Sue Park

This Newbery award-winning book is often recommended for younger kids, but teens will find it every bit as engaging. This is the story of Tree-ear, a thirteen-year-old orphan who is hired by the master potter, Min, in Korea during the twelfth century. It's a story of master and apprentice, both trying to prove themselves in the only way they know how. I think Linda Sue Park is one of today's best writers for children—this title is not to miss! Also try her other works, especially *A Long Walk to Water: Based on a True Story* (I share more about my experience reading it in chapter 5).

A Wrinkle in Time by Madeleine L'Engle

This book can be enjoyed by younger kids, but teens will find a lot to love as Meg and Charles embark on a quest through space to find their father. It's a story of good versus evil, of possibility, and coming-of-age. Smart and timeless, this book will likely become a family favorite. If your teens haven't read it before, reading it aloud to them will be a magical experience. If they have already read it on their own, they likely won't be opposed to you reading it aloud. Also try: other books by Madeleine L'Engle—I especially recommend *Meet the Austins*. Readers who enjoy the magical element of *A Wrinkle in Time* may also enjoy the work of Elizabeth Marie Pope in *The Sherwood Ring* and *The Perilous Gard*.

You Learn by Living: Eleven Keys to a More Fulfilling Life by Eleanor Roosevelt

Eleanor Roosevelt remains one of the most well-loved public figures in American history. In this wise and touching guide, she shares stories and wisdom about being a lifelong learner, fighting your fears, using time well, becoming mature, learning to be flexible, and more. "As I look back," she writes at the beginning of this book, "I think probably the fact which influenced me most in my early years was an avid desire, even before I was aware of what I was doing, to experience all I could as deeply as I could." And for the next two hundred or so pages, she describes exactly how we can do just that ourselves. Witty, humorous, and insightful, this little book will provide fodder for many discussions with your teens. For more inspiring non-fiction, also try: *How to Win Friends and Influence People* by Dale Carnegie, a fabulously entertaining book on people skills. You'll likely enjoy these books every bit as much as your teens.

ACKNOWLEDGMENTS

For each one of you, named and unnamed, who played a part in making this book come to life, I am so grateful. This book couldn't have been written without you.

Jim Trelease, thank you for stepping out in courage to write *The Read-Aloud Handbook*. A generation of families is changed because of it. Andrew Pudewa, thank you for lighting the spark and igniting a desire to read to my kids.

To my wonderful agent, Bill Jensen (and Sheila, whom I suspect is half the reason Bill is so wonderful), and the Zondervan team—especially Carolyn McCready, Harmony Harkema, Alicia Kasen, and Robin Barnett: thank you for believing in this book, sometimes more than I did. Thank you for telling me to try again when it wasn't working and for pulling out all the stops to get it to press so quickly. All of you are amazing.

Angela Fredericks, Natalie Schroeder, and all of the beautiful ladies from St. Joseph Homeschool Group: faithful friends through thick and thin. Pam Barnhill: my safe place and beloved friend. Anne Bogel: for keeping me sane and making me laugh. Rosalie Nourse: who loves my children every bit as a grandmother. Meghan Kunzl: loved dearly even from afar. Karla Marsh: lifelong and never-ending love and support. Mystie Winckler and Brandy Vencel: inspiring and unfailing friendship. C. S. Lewis said, "Friendship is unnecessary, like philosophy, like art . . . it has no survival value; rather it is one of those things which give value to survival." Indeed. I hope we share many more unnecessary moments.

Mom, Dad, Tiffany, Haylie, and all of your other halves and sweet children—the loss we grieved while I wrote these pages was larger than we thought we could bear. I love you. Dylan and Mikayla—I love you more than I've ever expressed. And I am so sorry for what you lost.

Ro, Randy, Angela, Dan, and all of your beautiful families, every bit as much my family as the one I was born into: thank you for loving me.

Thank you to Jodie Naker, who loves my children so well. The peace and joy you bring to our family is tangible.

Read-Aloud Revival community: this book would not exist without you. Your emails, letters, hugs, and encouragement are what make it a true revival. What began as a spark flamed into a roaring wildfire only because of your enthusiasm to connect with your kids through books. Thank you, thank you, thank you.

To the women who make *RAR* what it is: Kortney Garrison and Kara Anderson. Words cannot begin to express how grateful I am that you are in my life, the hands and feet keeping *RAR* on the right path. Thank you hardly feels like enough. I love you both.

And to the real heroes behind this book: my family. For keeping me in chocolate. For believing I could do it when I was sure I couldn't. For giving me the time and space even when there was none to spare. Every word in this book is because of you. Audrey, Allison, Drew, Clara Jane, Emerson, and Becket: my children, my heart. I love you one million sixty-six seventy-seven. I love you infinity.

Above all, my deepest gratitude goes to Andy: I don't know where to begin. I didn't deserve you and never will. I love you, Cal.

NOTES

Chapter 1: How Reading Aloud Can Change the World

1. JimTrelease, *The Read-Aloud Handbook*, (New York: Penguin Books, 2013), 4.
2. Ibid., 56.
3. N. D. Wilson, *Death by Living*, (Nashville: Thomas Nelson, 2013), 107.

Chapter 2: Waiting for the Walrus

1. Sarah Clarkson, interview by Sarah Mackenzie, *Read-Aloud Revival* podcast audio, Episode 17 "On Living a Storyformed Life," January 12, 2015, https://readaloudrevival.com/17/.
2. Tsh Oxenreider, interview by Sarah Mackenzie, *Read-Aloud Revival* podcast audio, Episode 3, "Reading Aloud Is Like Comfort Food," May 22, 2014, https://readaloudrevival.com/3/.

Chapter 3: Roar of the Lion

1. William Bennett, ed., *The Children's Book of Virtues*, (New York: Simon and Schuster, 1995), 84.
2. Kate Torgovnick May, "12 things I know for sure: Anne Lamott speaks at TED2017," *TEDblog*, accessed November 18, 2017, https://blog.ted.com/12-things-i-know-for-sure-anne-lamott-at-ted2017/.
3. Carolyn Leiloglou, interview by Sarah Mackenzie, *Read-Aloud Revival* podcast audio, Episode 41, "Navigating Fantasy: A Guide for Christian Parents," February 23, 2016, https://readaloudrevival.com/41/.

4. Jamie C. Martin, *Give Your Child the World: Raising Globally Minded Kids One Book at a Time* (Grand Rapids: Zondervan, 2016), 35.

5. Katherine Paterson, *A Sense of Wonder: On Reading and Writing Books for Children*, (New York: Plume, 1995), 67–68.

6. G. K. Chesterton, "The Ethics of Elfland," in *Orthodoxy* (New York: John Lane, 1908), 96.

7. C. S. Lewis, "Three Ways of Writing for Children," in *On Stories: and Other Essays on Literature* (San Diego: Harcourt, 1982), 39.

Chapter 4: Ready or Not

1. Jeanne Meister, "The Future of Work: Job-Hopping Is the 'New Normal' for Millennials," *Forbes*, August 14, 2012, accessed May 31, 2017, https://www.forbes.com/sites/jeannemeister/2012/08/14/the-future-of-work-job-hopping-is-the-new-normal-for-millennials/#2c69f90413b8.

2. Catherine Pakaluk, interview by Sarah Mackenzie, *Read-Aloud Revival* podcast audio, Episode 9, "A University Professor's Perspective on Reading Aloud," August 16, 2014, https://readaloud revival.com/9/.

3. Dr. Joseph Price, interview by Sarah Mackenzie, *Read-Aloud Revival* podcast audio, Episode 33, "The Research Behind Reading Aloud, Dr. Joseph Price," October 27, 2015 https://readaloudrevival .com/33/.

4. Trelease, *The Read-Aloud Handbook*, 4.

5. Ibid., 22.

6. Ibid., 15.

7. Andrew Pudewa, interview by Sarah Mackenzie, *Read-Aloud Revival* podcast audio, Episode 1, "Reading Aloud to Older Kids, A Conversation with Andrew Pudewa," April 27, 2014, https://read aloudrevival.com/1/.

8. Rebecca Bellingham, "Why We Should All Be Reading Aloud to Children, TEDx Youth @BeaconStreet, accessed June 1, 2017, https://www.youtube.com/watch?v=ZBuT2wdYtpM.

Chapter 5: Walking a Mile

1. Susan Schaeffer Macaulay, *For the Children's Sake: Foundations of Education for Home and School*, (Wheaton: Crossway Books, 1984), 112.

2. Sarah Caplan, "Does Reading Fiction Make You a Better Person?" *The Washington Post,* July 22, 2016, accessed June 3, 2017. https://www.washingtonpost.com/news/speaking-of-science/wp/2016/07/22/does-reading-fiction-make-you-a-better-person/.

3. Rudine Sims Bishop, "Mirrors, Windows, and Sliding Glass Doors," originally published in *Perspectives: Choosing and Using Books for the Classroom,* Vol. 6, Summer 1990, accessed on June 3, 2017. https://www.psdschools.org/webfm/8559.

4. Charlotte Mason, *School Education: Developing a Curriculum, AmblesideOnline's Annotated Charlotte Mason Series,* accessed June 3, 2017. https://www.amblesideonline.org/CM/vol3complete.html#3_16/.

5. Mark 12:30 (NIV).

6. Mark 12:31 (NIV).

7. Harper Lee, *To Kill a Mockingbird* (New York: Grand Central Publishing, 1982), 30.

8. Linda Sue Park, interview by Sarah Mackenzie, *Read-Aloud Revival* podcast audio, Episode 53 "Can a Children's Book Change the World?" October 30, 2016, https://readaloudrevival.com/53/.

Chapter 6: Create a Book Club Culture at Home

1. Trelease, *The Read-Aloud Handbook,* 1.

2. Daniel T. Willingham, *Raising Kids Who Read,* (San Franscisco: Jossey-Bass, 2015), 2.

3. Trelease, *The Read-Aloud Handbook,* 3.

4. Paterson, *A Sense of Wonder,* 30.

5. Willingham, *Raising Kids Who Read,* 4.

6. Alan Jacobs, *The Pleasures of Reading in an Age of Distraction,* (Oxford: Oxford University Press, 2011), 17.

7. Ibid.

8. Jonathan Auxier, interview by Sarah Mackenzie, *Read-Aloud Revival* podcast audio, Episode 56, "What's At Stake and Why Stories Matter," Nov. 29, 2016, https://readaloudrevival.com/56/.

9. Paterson, *A Sense of Wonder,* 59.

Chapter 7: Debunk Five Myths

1. Andrew Peterson, "A Note to Parents," *The Wingfeather Saga* (blog) accessed on June 8, 2017, http://wingfeathersaga.com/a-note-to-parents/.

2. Meg Meeker, "Spend More Time with Your Kids," *Meg Meeker, M.D.*, accessed on June 8, 2017. https://megmeekermd.com/blog/spend-more-time-with-your-kids/.

3. Ibid.

Chapter 9: Become a Literary Matchmaker

1. Jim Weiss, interview by Sarah Mackenzie, *Read-Aloud Revival* podcast audio, Episode 5, "The Importance of Reading Aloud Imperfectly," June 22, 2014, https://readaloudrevival.com/5/.

2. Laura Martin, interview by Sarah Mackenzie, *Read-Aloud Revival* podcast audio, Episode 64, "Helping Resistant Readers Fall in Love with Books, Laura Martin," May 9, 2017, https://readaloudrevival.com/64/.

Chapter 10: Master the Art of Conversation

1. Trelease, *The Read-Aloud Handbook*, 103.

2. Francis Bacon, *The Essays*, (USA: Renaissance Classics, 2012), 157.

3. Sally Lloyd Jones, interview by Sarah Mackenzie, *Read-Aloud Revival* podcast audio, Episode 60, "Your Job Is to Plant the Seed, a Conversation with Sally Lloyd Jones," March 13, 2017, https://readaloudrevival.com/60/.

Chapter 12: Books Are Delicious

1. Trelease, *The Read-Aloud Handbook*, 53.

2. MaryAnn F. Kohl, *Storybook Art: Hands-On Art for Children in the Styles of 100 Great Picture Book Illustrators* (Bellingham: Bright Ring Publishing, Inc., 2003), 75

Chapter 13: Age of Wonder

1. Trelease, *The Read-Aloud Handbook*, 10.

INDEX OF BOOKS BY TITLE

INDEX OF AUTHORS
AND ILLUSTRATORS

INDEX OF BOOKS BY AGE RECOMMENDATION

Ages 4–7

Ages 8–12

Ages 13+

RECOMMENDED RESOURCES FOR PARENTS

The Book Whisperer by Donalyn Miller

Books Children Love by Elizabeth Wilson

Caught Up in a Story: Fostering a Storyformed Life of Great books & Imagination with your Children by Sarah Clarkson

For the Children's Sake: Foundations of Education for Home and School by Susan Schaeffer Macaulay

Give Your Child the World: Raising Globally Minded Kids One Book at a Time by Jamie C. Martin

Honey for a Child's Heart by Gladys Hunt

Honey for a Teen's Heart by Gladys Hunt and Barbara Hampton

The Pleasures of Reading in an Age of Distraction by Alan Jacobs

Raising Kids Who Read by Dr. Daniel Willingham

The Read-Aloud Handbook by Jim Trelease

Read for the Heart by Sarah Clarkson

Reading in the Wild by Donalyn Miller

Reading Magic: Why Reading Aloud to Our Children Will Change Their Lives Forever by Mem Fox and Judy Horacek

The Reading Promise by Alice Ozma

A Sense of Wonder by Katherine Paterson *Note: Katherine Paterson's various essay collections are currently out of print, and therefore, difficult to find. If you'd like to hunt them down anyway, *The Invisible Child* (Dutton, 2001) contains a few essays from *A Sense of Wonder* and a few new essays as well.